SERMONS WHICH PROMPT, PROVOKE & PROMOTE LIFE

Living a Whole Life:

Sermons which Prompt, Provoke & Promote Life

Living a Whole Life:

Sermons which Prompt, Provoke & Promote Life

By

Minister Onedia N. Gage, Ph. D.

SERMONS WHICH PROMPT, PROVOKE & PROMOTE LIFE

GOD'S WORDS

Job 10:12

You gave me life and showed me kindness, and in your providence watched over my spirit.

Job 33:4

The Spirit of God has made me; the breath of the Almighty gives me life.

Psalm 23:6

Surely your goodness and love will follow me all the days of my life, and I will dwell in the house of the LORD forever.

Matthew 6:27

Can any one of you by worrying add a single hour to your life?

Matthew 10:39

Whoever finds their life will lose it, and whoever loses their life for my sake will find it.

John 13:38

Then Jesus answered, "Will you really lay down your life for me? Very truly I tell you, before the rooster crows, you will disown me three times!"

John 10:10

The thief cometh not, but for to steal, and to kill, and to destroy: I am come that they might have life, and that they might have it more abundantly.

Dedication

To those who are spiritually dead,

Who are in doubt about His power,

Who need to hear from God,

Who are emotionally paralyzed,

Who are mentally broken,

Who are burdened,

Who are weary,

Who are heavy laden,

And Living Out of the Will of God for Your Life.

Read this with the anticipation that you will LIVE again;

Leaving the dead of yourself behind;

Living Whole again.

OTHER BOOKS BY
MINISTER ONEDIA GAGE, PH. D.

90 Days of Powerful Words: Affirmations and Advice for Girls
Are You Ready for 9th Grade . . . Again? A Family's Guide to Success
As We Grow Together Daily Devotional for Expectant Couples
As We Grow Together Prayer Journal for Expectant Couples
As We Grow Together Her Workbook
As We Grow Together His Workbook
The Best 40 Days of Your Life: A Journey of Spiritual Renewal
The Blue Print: Poetry for the Soul
From Fat to Fit in 90 Days: A Fitness Journal
From Two to One: The Notebook for the Christian Couple
Hannah's Voice: Powerful Lessons in Prayer
Her Story The Legacy of Her Fight: The Bible Study
Her Story The Legacy of Her Fight: The Devotional
Her Story The Legacy of Her Fight: The Legacy Journal
Her Story The Legacy of Her Fight: Prayers and Journal
ILY! A Mother Daughter Relationship Workbook
In Her Own Words: Notebook for the Christian Woman
In Purple Ink: Poetry for the Spirit
The Intensive Retreat for Couples for Her
The Intensive Retreat for Couples for Him
Love Letters to God from a Teenage Girl
The Measure of a Woman: The Details of Her Soul
The Notebook: For Me, About Me, By Me
The Notebook for the Christian Teen
On This Journey Daily Devotional for Young People
On This Journey Prayer Journal for Young People
On This Journey Prayer Journal for Young People, Vol 2
One Day More Than We Deserve Prayer Journal for the Growing Christian
Promises, Promises: A Christian Novel
Queen in the Making: 30 Week Bible Study for Teen Girls
She Spoke Volumes . . . And Then Some
Six Months of Solitude: The Sanctity of Singleness Notebook
Tools for These Times: Timely Sermons for Uncertain Times
With An Anointed Voice: The Power of Prayer
Yielded and Submitted: A Woman's Journey for a Life Dedicated to God
Yielded and Submitted: A Woman's Journey for a Life Dedicated to God Intimate Study
Yielded and Submitted: A Woman's Journey for a Life Dedicated to God Prayers and Journal

LIBRARY OF CONGRESS

Living a Whole Life:

Sermons which Prompt, Provoke and Promote Life

All Rights Reserved © 2017

Rev. Onedia N. Gage, Ph. D.

No part of this of book may be reproduced or transmitted in Any form or by any means, graphic, electronic, or mechanical, Including photocopying, recording, taping, or by any Information storage or retrieval system, without the Permission in writing from the publisher.

Purple Ink, Inc. Press

For Information address:
Purple Ink, Inc.
P O Box 300113
Houston, TX 77230
www.purpleink.net
onediagage@purpleink.net

Onedia Gage Ministries

www.onediagage.com
onediagage@onediagage.com

ISBN:

978-1-939119-30-8

Printed in United States

Dear God,

I am thankful for Your gift and Your anointing. I am thinking that You have given me these gifts to share with others. I am thankful that I am chosen for the work You have given me to do. I hope that I am making You proud at least 10% of the time that I am in Your service. I can only thank You for holding me and my life together in such a manner that I am able to walk before You in a pleasing manner.

Lord, I meet so many broken people and I know that You are the Author and Finisher of our faith. They break my heart. I am ever grateful that You are the lifter of my head and my plans You have for me.

Thank You for the title of this work. Living a Whole Life is certainly a gift You gave me when I was LOW. In a season of pain and of bleakness, I surrendered to You and You spoke to me. Hearing Your voice was my source of hope in my hopelessness.

As You use these words and this vessel for Your benefit, I am ever mindful that You had a choice in who delivered this message, so I am thankful that You chose me. In this walk with You, I am hopeful that I can be forgiven for disappointing You.

Lord, I hope that the message is clear and as profound as You gave it to me.

Lord, I thank You lastly for the gift of preaching as I live to serve You.

Your daughter,

Onedia

Dear Father God,

Oh Lord, Our Lord, how excellent is Thy name in all the Earth!

Lord, I bless and adore You this day and pray that You forgive me of my sins. I am committed to the work You have for me. I am continually trying to figure out how to love You more and serve You better.

As I walk each day help me to discern the enemy and its schemes against me, as it tries to overcome You. Lord, I want to be in the tune to the Holy Spirit such that I can hear the guidance and direction You offer to me through the Holy Spirit. Remind me to give You all of the honor, glory and praise for those things I ask and that come into fruition because it is Your will.

I am overwhelmed Lord when You just show up and do exceedingly, abundantly, more than I can ask or think. I am sure of my election. Help me remain steadfast in that choice: to serve You for the rest of my life. Likewise, Master, I am in need of insuring that I am protected from the enemy at all times so that I do not fall across enemy lines.

Lord, I am aware of the journey that I am on and its challenges. Thank You for giving me the armor and perseverance and the will to continue on the path for You, the one of righteousness and not evil. Thank You for the sensitivity that is required to serve others. May I be able to understand why they are in my path and that I serve them appropriately.

Thank You for those who will read these pages and be saved, helped, and rescued. I pray that hey deepen their relationship with You. They will then know You personally in the pardon of their sins. I look forward to the next assignment.

In Jesus' name, I pray these blessings.

Amen.

Dear Sister and Brother,

I pray that this finds you well! I am praying for you as you seek a deeper relationship with Christ! I do not know the crossroads of your life at this time, however, I am in a personal storm. At this time of this writing, I am homeless. I am living at my grandmother's house and she is being unwelcoming. I share not to draw your sympathy. I share this to let you know that God has not forgotten about you.

God has not forgotten that I have been unemployed for two years, having financial issues, no longer qualify for unemployment payments, and having trouble getting independent assignments to sustain myself. God is present and holding me together. God is calling me pay attention to Him during this time. You may be thinking this is easy for me. However, I still pray and meditate and study. I still ask the same questions you do. I have the same concerns that you do.

God is there and is aware of your situation. I want to give up from time to time and to throw in the towel. Instead, I stay the course and remain steadfast, waiting faithfully on God.

I pray that these sermons meet your needs. I pray that they help you find resolve. I pray that they offer you peace and comfort. I pray that they call you out of your rut and challenge you to meet the needs you can and that they remind you to run to God.

This is God's time. When you are at your weakest, then God is at His strongest. Because that is when you allow Him the ability to do His work, His best work.

I am praying for you as I mentioned. I am prayerful that you seek God and surrender yourself unto Him, invoke and investigate your heart's deterioration so that God can restore you to Him, and meditate on and meddle in the business that God has for you. Why does God have you 'here?' Seek Him for answers but with the understanding that you are asking Him for His will, not your wish list.

I implore you to ask God what He wants you to learn and how He wants you to grow. I am confident that He will hear you and your situation will reach a resolve.

So take courage. This walk is not for the weak or the faint at heart. God equips those who serve Him with unbelievable strength and in stormy times, we need all of it. We just have to remember that our strength is only available by accessing Him. We are HIS vessels, His sheep, the sheep of His pasture. We live, breath, serve, preach, teach, and are anointed at His command, for His pleasure, and His use alone. WE need to be mindful of that as we progress in this life.

Living a Whole Life is for you to grow to seek God and all of His characteristics. This is not a dress rehearsal. This is the real thing. We are in need of direction, guidance, encouragement, and love. We need all of these things from Him. God is the only One who can do all of those things at the same time and do them all well at the same time.

Thank you for taking this journey with me. It is sometimes lonely, always exciting, and most of all the best choice you can make in your life. Read each scripture passage with the anticipation that God has provided you with the living water for the thirst you have. Read each sermon expecting that God will meet you there at the very point of your need. Read each prayer knowing that God has prepared it just for you and your current situation. Allow all of the words to penetrate your heart so that you can move forward and do the work that God has called you to do.

I pray that your needs are met and that these words minister to your heart, mind, and spirit in such a profound manner that you know that you had a personal encounter with God.

I pray that you remain focused.

In God's Service,

Onedia N. Gage

Onedia N. Gage

Table of Contents

Dedication — 9

Prayer — 13

Sermons — 23

    Some Powerful Tears
    John 11:35
    25

    There Should Be Some Evidence
    John 15:1-4; 1 John 2:3-6
    39

    Love Without Hypocrisy
    Exodus 34:5-7
    51

    Anger is Real and Does Not Have to Cost
    Ephesians 4:26-27
    63

    Do You Hear the Words Coming Out of My Mouth
    Ephesians 4:29
    77

    A Sacrificial Love
    Ephesians 5:25-30
    87

    A Sign, A Signal, and A Solution
    Exodus 40:33-38
    99

    Across Enemy Lines
    Ephesians 6:10-12
    111

An Upgrade of Your Faith
Hebrews 11:1-10
121

A Life Changing Walk
Matthew 14:22-36
131

A Good Definition of Nothing
Psalm 16:2; John 15:5; 1 Corinthians 13:2-3
145

That You Might Endure
James 1:2-4
155

It is My Day to Watch Them
Genesis 4:9
165

With His Hands
John 20:24-31
169

Some Unresponsive Clay
Isaiah 29:16; 45:9, 64:8
181

With a Dirty Heart and Some Horrible Motives
Romans 7:9-25
203

Acknowledgements   215

About the Minister   217

Living A Whole Life:

Sermons which Prompt, Provoke & Promote Life

SOME POWERFUL TEARS
JOHN 11:35

Jesus wept.

John 11:35 (NIV)

We had a family tradition that we recited a scripture after my grandmother prays over the meals. Well, my sister always said 'Jesus swept' or so I thought. It sounded to me that Jesus was sweeping. I never understood and I did not feel like I should ask her what verse she was using. But for many years, she would say that and I would think that Jesus was sweeping.

As I mentioned, I was completely unclear about the sweeping she claimed that Jesus was doing. It just seemed to me that she did not have a good grasp of the Bible so she said He swept. And I couldn't believe that Jesus was in the Bible sweeping. It was just impossible for me to believe that He would be sweeping. But one day, as I was reading the Bible, I came across those words: Jesus wept. At the time I came across them, I just cried and cried and cried. If I had known earlier that she was trying to say that He had wept, I would have felt a lot better about myself.

The context of our scripture text today comes from the fact that Lazarus had gotten sick. And Mary and Martha were his sisters and they sent word to Jesus that he was sick. And when they had sent the word that he was sick, Jesus remained ministering where He was for two additional days. Between the time Jesus got the word and the time that He was able to make His way to Lazarus, Lazarus died. Until Jesus got to Lazarus, Martha and Mary worried. Martha had her normal rant when Jesus arrived, 'If You had been here, if only You had been here earlier.'

And then upon understanding the whole context surrounding Lazarus' death, Jesus weeps. And then after He wept, He called Lazarus forward out of the grave. Lazarus was resurrected. Now, Jesus prays to His Father that You have heard Me, Lord. He prays to Him and tells Him, 'You heard Me, Lord.' Because of that, then we can then say that God is listening to us. God hears us. God honors our requests. This text teaches us several things.

CARE FOR OTHERS

Jesus teaches us to care for others and pray for others and the ultimate compassion for others. Now, we talk about caring for other people. We sometimes put a condition on them. Our compassion has conditional statements. We are going to care for them until 'this' happens. We are going to care for them under these conditions or circumstances occur. We are going to care for them at this particular point in time. We are going to care for them, but differently. It is the point in which we care for them like Jesus said to care for them. Then we are doing what it is He says and what He would do.

Now, here's why we have to care for others. Although there are some instructions Jesus gives us, He says we need to care for one another. These instructions are under that umbrella of love one another. Those two go together. 'How long am I supposed to care about them?' And I want to be sure that I make it clear that we have to care for others as long as we are alive, period. I did not say alive and well. I said alive.

'Well, for me that is just not right. I cannot do all that. What do you expect of me?' Well, I am not expecting anything of you. However, Jesus is expecting us to care for those to whom we are assigned and to who are assigned to us. Now, we reassign ourselves regularly. And I want to be real clear about this, if we reassign ourselves regularly because we think that we can just do whatever we want, and that we do not have to care for people. It is subjective and is based on our conditions and what our personal needs are. But those are the things that do not have anything to do with care. We have to care for others and we are assigned to certain people for whom to care for them.

"Well, that is just not right.' And then we introduce the 'what if.' The what if list can be very long and very detailed. Here's the problem with that attitude and activity. We are assigned to care for other people. It is a non-negotiable assignment. When we care for others, it includes wiping their tears, handling their fears, managing their doubt, sharing our testimony, and helping them be encouraged. It is those things we are assigned to do. I am not asking you if you feel like it, or if you thought about wanting to do it. I'm not asking you any of that. I'm telling you that it is your just and due assignment.

'Well, that is just not right.' I understand you may not feel it is right. However, it is your assignment. And what you need to realize is this is something you're going to need to get accomplished. Otherwise, you won't succeed and will continue to be on that same assignment. It is not going to stop. Now, I understand we often use the 'reap what you sow' concept when someone does something bad. We want others to reap the evil that they have done to us, repaid to us. Likewise, it should be the good that you have done to be repaid you as well. But do be careful wishing that others reap what they sow for grace is built on not getting what we truly deserve. What you do not want to happen to yourself, you should not want for others, even if they have wronged you.

You do not have any idea when you will stand in need of another individual. So, it should occur to you likewise to pay it forward, so you do not run into those types of scenarios. We all will come in need of things from time to time. And you are assigned to somebody like somebody is assigned to you. It just behooves you to pay attention at the level which you can focus on caring for another person, and putting your selfishness aside. This is an exercise of whether you can relinquish your selfishness.

'Well, I am not selfish. I give all the time.' But you give under your conditions. You do that when it is at your convenience. It is when you feel like it. You will need to be able to care when it is not at your convenience. We give money when it is convenient. We give money because something happened. We do those things at our leisure. However, why do not you care for someone when it is not convenient? Can you care for someone when it is not convenient? Can you care for someone when it does not meet your needs? It does not cover what your concerns are?

Can you do that? And the likelihood is that we have a problem with that. We have a problem with caring for others on their terms, when they need us, how they need us. It doesn't have anything to do what you want and when you want it. It is based on what you need to do because God is asking it of you at that time. He put a person, a human being in front of your situation with a human condition in front of you in order for you to serve Him. Yes, He did. It is the test of will you do it.

Can He trust you to do it? And if the answer is no, then we have got to discuss what we are going to do next. Because the whole goal is can you be mature enough? Or do you want to be mature enough to handle what God has assigned to you?

CONCERN FOR OTHERS

Now, our next point is concern for others. We should have a genuine concern and care for another person. And I do not only mean, are you concerned about their well-being. Yes, I mean that. I mean are you concerned about them, deeply concerned? What does deep concern mean? Well, as we define deep concern, it involves understanding that this person is going to need you regardless of what they do or do not do. You see, sometimes a person you have to care and have concern for are not going to be grateful for what you will do.

Mothers complain about this constantly. They always say, 'well my kids are ungrateful, and my kids do not appreciate me, my kids . . . .' They have this long list of things their kids do not do and what their kids are not. I asked those moms, "Did you share with them how to be grateful and what did grateful look like?" 'Well, what do you mean?' "Well, if you want them to appreciate you, then what does that look like?" "When I say I want my child to appreciate me that means I want my children to say thank you, and please and excuse me."

But I want every person to say that, it does not matter who you are. I want you to say those things. And when I do something for you, you do not owe me anything. It is not to be mentioned again. People sometimes keep into their mindset that if I've done something to you or for you then you owe me something; that you're designed to give me something. That actually is not the case because your service is unto the Lord. It has nothing to do with this other individual. It has nothing to do with who they are, what they can do for you. It is you gave something of yourself, of your resources that have been given to you to give to them.

You were assigned some resources only because certain people are going to cross your path who are going to need what it is you have. You are given it for them not for yourself. When you do not give them those resources, those resources will then reassigned to someone else or they're just simply unassigned to you. And that sounds very harsh, but here's the thing, we are blessed, so that we are to be blessings to other people. We are blessed to be blessings to other people.

God blesses who He can send blessings through. If you're going be the stop gap, if you shut the blessings down, the blessing cycle, then you won't be included in the cycle, period. It is as simple as that. When we talk about the blessing cycle; people get nervous and concerned and confused, the problem with that is this, you got to ask yourself if you needed something, would you want someone else holding your blessings hostage?

And do you want to be concerned about something when the concern is to be based on what God has wanted to do for you. It is not based on this. It is based on the fact that He did already enough for you. He thought enough of you to bless you. He thought enough of you to give to you. He thought enough of you to too consider you.

People ask, 'What does that look like?' When people tell me that the man on the corner might use the money on alcohol. 'Well, you know what, that is too bad.' 'Well, do you give money him all the time?' 'No, because I do not always have money. But if I have a bag of food I just bought from the store, I'm going to give it to that person. If I have a bottle of water in my car which I normally have, I'm going to give it to that person.'

Because God says when you serve the least of these, you serve Me. I give you what I have or what I'm available to give you. I'll give it to you freely. I'm not going to lecture you. I'm not going to ask you. But I'm not going to give to you my leftovers either. I'm not going to give you something that I wouldn't accept or I would not feel right in giving away. I give my best because I do not want God to come back and say, 'Is that the best you could do for My servant? That was the best you had?'

I do not want God to say, "That is not the best you had. Let me show you the best you had." And that right there, that conversation, I would always want to avoid that because that one brings me to tears. "Because you should always do better. And you shall begin doing better. You chose against doing better, Onedia." And I do not want to hear God say those words to me. I do not want that to resonate in my spirit. For that reason, I'm compelled to do the right thing right away. So, if I do the right thing as far as to not to have to be in the chastisement then I can move on with my day. I can move on freely and clear spirited, because I know I did the right thing upfront.

Care or concern can get cumbersome. I understand that. 'I'm always the one giving. I'm always the one that has to do the right thing.' Amen. Because you can be trusted. And He wants to continue to trust you. This is not a good time to sacrifice the trust God has in you. You also need to remember this is your time to grow. You need to realize what you can be trusted with. There were times before your maturity that you knew you could not be trusted to do certain things. Now, you know some of what you can be trusted with. This only comes with practice. If you are broken or you're feeling empty and you want to be full and you want to have some help with it, then why do not you ask God for that?

Ask God to replenish you to the level that you can feel Him again, and where you can understand that He's loving you in a fashion that says, 'Lord, I'm being loved right now by You. And while I'm not feeling any human hands, You're loving me right now.' Ask Him. Because what we are not going to be able to do is change how we are to care for and have concerns for other people nor we can change who those persons are to whom we are responsible. We cannot change any of those things. Those are not within our control.

I do not believe that God will answer you if you asked to be relieved of those particular responsibilities. Let's talk about Nathan and David (2 Samuel 2).

Nathan is assigned to David. Nathan presents David with a scenario, and says to David, what would you do if? David proposed a very harsh punishment. Nathan responds, 'Well it was you. So now, what we are going to do?' Don't you think Nathan wanted to be excused from that particular assignment? Because Nathan is talking to the King, who has the power to strike him dead on the spot. A man that God picked to rule His personal nation.

Or maybe it is Ananias (Acts 9) that you better identify with. When Ananias is assigned to Saul who is being brought to Jesus in his own special way, Ananias rejected that assignment, immediately. 'Excuse me God, no. That is a murderer. I am not going to talk to him.' But Jesus said, 'I got this.' You're on assignment to care and be concerned for another person. And it is not something you can reject. It is not something you can partially accept. It is not possible at all.

Please get past the mindset that this is negotiable because it is not. You cannot negotiate with God on how you can have care and concern for another individual. It is just not possible. We need to realize and recognize is this, we cannot give to someone else what belongs to God, who has assigned it to a special person. You cannot give it away to somebody else. It is for whom He has assigned it to through you. You cannot trade them and ask God for someone different. That is not acceptable.

COMPASSION FOR OTHERS

Care and concern should lead to compassion. Now, I want us to understand in these Bible verses what has transpired. Lazarus is dead. Jesus is weeping because this is Jesus' uncle.

Now, when Jesus asked God to be glorified in this scenario and listen to Him and He raises Lazarus from the dead, He cried but He already knew what was going to happen. He knew He was going to raise Lazarus from the dead. But He cried anyway. And that is the ultimate compassion; in front of Martha and Mary. What is it costing you to be compassionate? And the answer is nothing.

It doesn't cost you anything to be compassionate. It doesn't cost you anything to offer what you have to another person. It is designed for us to be able to sacrifice our pride and do the right thing by giving of ourselves to other people. For those other people who gave a lot of themselves to us, and it is a remarkable thing. We cannot figure that out for the life of us how to really make compassion manifest itself. We want to be able to do all these things but we cannot, for the life of us, get this together where we can say to ourselves, 'hey self I need to be compassionate to another person.' And definitely without asking what's in it for me.

The interesting thing about us is as human beings, we want to know exactly what you're going through before we can be compassionate to another person's situation. And that should not be required. I should be able to tell you I'm having trouble and that is enough for your give over your compassion to me. You should be able to look at me and just be compassionate just because. Just because! If you know this as my normal behavior then something changes, then you should be compassionate just because.

Not for any other reason other than to say, I am being compassionate to you because of who you are, period, to me and otherwise, but we get beside ourselves. We are judgmental, 'She did not say all of what she was going through. She was just acting differently.' Why is that okay? Why is it okay for you to just act as if she has to tell you everything single thing that is going on with her or him for you to say, 'oh, well, I did not know.' You did not need to know. Just as a side bar: Have you ever considered why she did not tell you everything? Did it occur to you that you cannot be trusted to hold that information in the strictest confidence? Is that the reason why she did not disclose her disease or her financial troubles to you? Did it occur to you that you still would not have helped her even if you did know everything that she was in need of? Your assignment is to be compassionate, to have care, and concern for another individual at all times regardless. Treat people kindly, period.

Ephesians chapter 4, verse 32 reads, "Be kind and compassionate to one another, forgiving one other, just as in Christ God forgave you." Treat other people like you want to be treated. When you go before the Lord and ask for compassion for your situation yet you are not compassionate to people He sends you, how likely is it that God will be compassionate to you? Not so much. And why should we expect Him to do so?

What has to happen so that we can decide that it is good enough to be given an assignment from God? You should be able to say, 'I'm going to be compassionate to him, another individual regardless of their situation, regardless of what I know because that is all we are dealing with it is what I know.' What you know should not be the driving factor of you being able to be compassionate to another individual.

You should be able to be compassionate to another person regardless of what it is you know and you do not know. You should be able to say, 'I'm going to give to you what I have because I have it, and you need it.' The other thing is not waiting for people to ask things of you. If you see them in need of something, you should just step right in and say, 'I see that you need this, here it is.' We need position ourselves to be available to be compassionate at the level that Jesus would. Will we ever reach His level? Maybe not. We need to give our best effort towards doing what it is He has asked and called us to do. What does compassionate look like?

Compassionate looks like a hug. Compassionate looks like a conversation when you listen, when you just listen to the other person, You listen to what they have to say, when I interrupting and without 'me-too-ing.' 'Me-too-ing' means, 'yeah, I'm having a hard time too,' and you take over their story and their time to share. This wasn't about you. This was about them. Let them finish and let them have their turn and their say. Let them finish the conversation and then you can say 'I had a similar situation as well.'

But there are times when you just have to say nothing. This is not your time to talk. This is not your time to speak. It is the other person's time to speak. So you let them talk and then you just say nothing. I had a person who I used to say that she was my friend. There's never been a situation where she listened to what I said about my issues. And finally, I had to say to myself, I am a friend to her. But she's not necessarily a friend to me. I'm on assignment to her to listen to her, to provide solutions for her, and to relay information to her.

Now, eventually we stopped communicating because that season was over. I wasn't upset because I know what I'm assigned to do. I understood that I'm on a specific assignment. And on my specific assignment, sometimes it is going to be a situation where I may not get what I thought I wanted out of the relationship. But it may not have been assigned that way. God may not have assigned us to be in that type of relationship with that person at that time.

In the event that you get into that scenario, remember 'why am I here? Why is this person in my life?' You can ask that question of God: 'why is this person in my life? Why am I in their life?' Be ready and wait on that answer. It might not always sound like you want it to sound. It may not always be what you want it to be. But at the end of the day, the Lord is going to get the glory and that is who is important in this whole situation. If God used you to bring light to another individual, then that was what you were assigned to do. That was your job. Accept your assignment from Jesus and keep it moving.

Why would you say that? That is all unfair. Really? Is it truly unfair? Is it really what you want to call unfair? Is that what you want to tell God? 'I think You're being unfair right now.' I do not think we want to go down that road. Was it fair when He forgave us for things we intentionally did? Was it fair when He gave us things we did not deserve? Was it fair when He gave us completely unmerited favor? It wasn't fair when Jesus got up on that cross. But He did it anyway. Jesus did not deserve to be on that cross. That was not fair. Fair means a cross for each of us, which was executed by someone who deserved to be on a cross on the side of me.

So, the point is God's assignments do not always appear fair. But have you always been fair? Have you always done the right thing in the relationship? Have you always given all that you were supposed to give to another individual? If the answer to any of that is no, then guess what? Then it was unfair to someone else. Consider our behavior and activities before we launch the 'It is Not Fair Campaign, Lord, And Why is This Happening To me?'

Let's be careful: someone is assigned to be compassionate to you. Someone is assigned to take care of you as well. There is an assignment out there that has your name on it and it has somebody attached to it. There is someone assigned to me who will say we will be compassionate to Onedia. There's a group of people assigned to me for that. And based on what we know, that assignment comes in God's time. It has nothing to do with me. I cannot even change it.

It has everything to do with the people who are assigned, their obedience. I am just a vessel that God uses to allow other people to progress in their maturity for Him. He wants to know will you do it. Can I trust you to be compassionate to her? Can I trust you to do the things I have called on you to do? Can I trust you to do these things? The answer is going to show through your behavior. Are you willing to give of yourself freely and openly? Because it is what God assigned you to do. Are you willing to do it?

If you're willing to do it, then fine. If you're not willing to do it, then He'll be aware of it. He'll be made aware and you'll be made aware as well. So do not ever think that you're not on a specific assignment, and that you're not under a specific umbrella of things you need to do just because God says to do it. You're on that assignment. And there's nothing that can take you away from it unless God changes His mind. And since that is not happening anytime real soon, you have to ask yourself, 'what am I supposed to be doing in the process? How am I supposed to be responding in the process? What am I supposed to be doing in the process so that I can be sure that I'm going to follow the directions that God has given to me?' I am grateful to those who are compassionate to me.

God is looking for those whom He created who are willing to serve through all circumstances. Are you that servant? Will you be like Jesus?

Care.

Concern.

Compassion.

Amen.

Our God, how we thank You, how we love You on this day. We thank You for Jesus dying on the cross and being resurrected for our sins. And Lord God, we thank You for the message and compassion He teaches us, shows us, shared with us each and every single day. And Lord God, right now, we thank You afresh for those of who call on us to be compassionate, caring, concerned for them. And that we will be able to be the wiser as far as what we will do and what it is You want to be able to do.

So Lord God, I thank You all for using me, assigning me to persons, and assigning persons to me, to whom I can have care and concern and compassion for in an overwhelming Jesus likewise fashion. And Lord, remind me when I'm not doing exactly what You call on me to do because I, Lord, want to follow You each day. Oh Lord, allow the person to hear this message, to follow You this way. Clean up our hearts to urge us in the spirit of our conviction to do exactly what You taught us to do.

So Lord God, I thank You afresh again and being able to forgive us all our sins and encourage us, to love us completely in a condition to keep us from all hurt, harm and danger. We thank You so much to all people who come in our path allow us with fresh eyes, to see them, of You who sent them to us to be and to be taken care of unconditionally under Your compassion through the power and blessings You give us. It is in Jesus name we pray that you bless us. Amen.

There Should Be Some Evidence
John 15: 1 – 4, 1 John 2:3 – 6, Mark 6:51

"I am the true vine, and my Father is the gardener. ² He cuts off every branch in me that bears no fruit, while every branch that does bear fruit he prunes so that it will be even more fruitful. ³ You are already clean because of the word I have spoken to you. ⁴ Remain in me, as I also remain in you. No branch can bear fruit by itself; it must remain in the vine. Neither can you bear fruit unless you remain in me.

John 15: 1 – 4 NIV

³ We know that we have come to know Him if we keep His commands. ⁴ Whoever says, "I know Him," but does not do what He commands is a liar, and the truth is not in that person. ⁵ But if anyone obeys His word, love for God is truly made complete in them. This is how we know we are in Him: ⁶ Whoever claims to live in Him must live as Jesus did.

1 John 2: 3 – 6 (NIV)

⁵¹ Then He climbed into the boat with them, and the wind died down. They were completely amazed,

Mark 6:51 (NIV)

Father God, right now I thank You in the name of Jesus for this time that we are sharing together. A time that we can just spend with You, Lord God for affirmation and knowledge and information and covering and just loving us the way You do. Lord God, I thank You right now that You are the keeper of our spirits and soul. You are the lifter of our heads and You are the One that strengthens our faith. Lord, we thank You right now; without You where would I be? Lord, certainly there will be some time we will surely mess up as we do all the time. Lord God, I thank You right now for forgiving us of our sins. Thank You for removing the desire of sin away from us. Thank You for all the things You brought our way. Thank You for this place in this world today Lord God. Father thank You right now for choosing to do exactly what You have determined that You would do and deciding that we need them today, In Jesus name we pray, and ask His blessings, Amen.

Our sermon topic is There Should Be Some Evidence. Have you ever paid attention to Matthew chapter 14, verse 30, which points out that Peter saw the winds? Have you ever seen wind? Have you ever seen wind? Matthew chapter 14, verse 30 reads: "But when he saw the winds, he was afraid and began to sink cried out, Lord save me."

How do we know the wind is real if we do not see it?

Everybody has not seen the wind, but we know it exists. What is the evidence we have that the wind is real? Although the wind is transparent, the wind has strength. The wind can change the demeanor of furniture, cars and other things, like light poles and other signs that were previously rooted in the cement and soil, even 100 year old trees. There is a video evidence of 100 year old tree and homes which have been moved and uprooted by a transparent, strong and immeasurable force better known as wind.

There is an instrument which can be used to estimate the speed of that wind, but there is no measurement for the power it has or the damage it is about to cause. Hurricane strength is a determined in part by wind and strength. 2012 marked the unique hurricane season defined by Hurricane Sandy. The Hurricane Sandy actually hit New Jersey and the surrounding areas. This was unique because it was partnered with a blizzard; it came suddenly there after, and the damage to those parts of New Jersey was very devastating. One of the costliest storms, into the billions, ever in history. Now understand, hurricanes are not new to anybody. We have heard about them or we have seen them or we have been a part of them or we have been placed or displaced by them, however, we try to understand the weight of their messes.

The wind speed dictates the category of the hurricane. The hurricanes are labeled category one to category five. At category five, hurricanes have been measured winds up of 195 miles per hour. This is certain to take out, destroy, damage and cause imminent harm to whatever is in its path. It is not a question of will it do damage, it is a question of how much damage will it do and how long can we sustain the amount of damage that will incur.

The point that I am making here is that there is evidence of the wind. You do not have to ask yourself was there a wind, or do you think there was a wind. It is not was or is, it is! It was here and this is how we know. That evidence of the wind comes via the damage it has done. So we cannot misunderstand and we cannot misinterpret it and we cannot be confused because we have evidence to understand. There is wind and there is evidence of the wind. There is the damage that it has done and the evidence is the clean-up that has to be done after that wind because of what has transpired. We have to ask ourselves how do we know that wind would cause this much damage? Well, all in all you want to be sure that you realize they inside of the wind situation, there is evidence.

Now, our scripture text teaches us that if we remain in Him, He remains in us. He likens Himself to and He metaphorically refers to Himself as The Vine and the Father as the Gardner. I do not know how much you know about horticulture or horticulturalism, but I am not a green thumb. I can grow and water a plant, but there is nothing that will sustain my interest for a long period of time.

However, a lot of people do this and they do this for a living; they have green houses and they have miles of vegetation. They have all kinds of things which help them to deliver the kind of greenery that we enjoy.

Presence

The first thing is that there is a presence in your life. This Presence is something that we cannot take for granted nor can we misunderstand or understate it. Realize that there is God's presence in our lives, Jesus' living presence in our lives, and the Holy Spirit is presence in our lives, and there should be some evidence of Their Presence. So we get confused, He may metaphorically describe Himself as a Vine, and His Father is the Gardner, but realizing that the vine He speaks of is a very healthy and very hard, not a wimpy tree; it is not the smallest branch, it is something very veined. I envisioned it as something with many intertwined veins. These trees are very old and very strong trees, there are many veins and there are many threads of strength interwoven into that tree.

It looks like it would take a miracle to chop it down. I mentioned earlier that there would be winds that will take them out of the ground, but there is no such wind that will take Jesus out of the vine, or out of the role of vine because He is assigned as the Vine. The Word says that if we remain in Him and He was to remain in us, then we would bear fruit. This fruit that we talked about and again metaphorically speaking: this fruit relies on us. The fruit is the evidence of us being relied upon to create disciples, to educate others, to introduce others to Christ, to share our faith with all people around us, and it will help us increase our own faith as well as the faith of others around us. So we have to ask ourselves what fruit are we producing, and are we not producing fruit that are not on the Vine, or we have rejected the teaching of the Vine, or is it because we have just decided we have a better way than the Vine. Well, understand that He is the true Vine, and in order to produce fruit, we have to stay connected to the Vine. He is very clear about that process.

What happens when we take an orange off the tree? Well, that orange that you have taken off the tree stops growing. There is evidence that it stops growing right there. Can it sustain for a specified period of time? Will it remain fresh in order for you to consume it? Well, you do have a short window of time to figure how you are going to accomplish it, and indeed, it will be a very short window. That short window is not going to allow for you to tarry very along. Oranges, theoretically last in my refrigerator probably a week and a half, maybe ten days. If it is not consumed within those 10 days, they are thrown away. At that point, they are no longer healthy to eat; they are no longer healthy to partake of, and because we know this, we then can go on to say, "Well I need to get into the position to produce fruit, I want to produce fruit."

There should be some evidence that God is in my life and that His presence is what produces the fruit. What that looks like is that I am going to share the word of God with others. I am going to be a disciple who can help others, and help others to become disciples as well. On top of that, I am also going to put myself in a position where I look like Christ. That fruit is what is going to provide that evidence. So when He is present in me, there are going to be things that I do, there are going to be things that I accomplish, there are going to be things that look like Him that I do. I should be like Him and I should understand Him. I should be able to be available to Him, and because I am available to Him, then there are things that I want to show evidence of. For example, Jesus being who He is, I should be producing disciples as a part of that fruit and part of His presence in my life. I should be fruitful myself, not only helping others to produce the fruits that should be produced, I should also be doing that. Let us talk about what I mean specifically.

Let us understand that we have spiritual gifts. Part of me being in God and God being in me and my believing in Him is that I should be able to use the gift that He has given me in order to produce some products. Well what I do know is that part of my gift is to preach, part of what I am to produce is to preach on His behalf, preach because of whom He is, preach because I love Him, preach because it is my gift, and it is my calling.

Second gift is teaching. I should be teaching on a regular basis in a classroom setting, small or otherwise, the word of God. And then lastly, and not comprehensively speaking, one of my gifts is writing, so I need to be producing things that give way and share my gift to be able to write to that end, I have published thirty-two books so far, with more to come this year. Understanding that when you consider where we are in our lives and what it is we are to be doing, we want to make sure and absolutely positively sure that we are producing the fruit that He has in mind. There is no way around it, you cannot get past it. You will either produce good fruit or be cut from the vine. Every farmer would agree. Every gardener would agree.

He also says as you produce fruit, you would be pruned, which means that extra stuff would be taken off and we are going to cut to the best part of the branch so you can produce a better branch because you have been cut back. It is an humbling mechanism. It is an understanding of who you are and what it is you are responsible for doing. It is part of who we are. It is what He does so we can stay focused on Him. This is what He does so that we can stay in tune with what He wants us to do. Understand that it is not you by yourself, it is everybody; everybody who He loves He is going to be pruned and anybody who is in Him, He is going to prune. Now if you are not of Him, and if you are just causing havoc, then you'll be cut away because you are not producing fruit. You are not adding to Him. You are not adding to the net worth or glory of God. That is very important and very critical to what we do and how we do what we do.

Purpose

Now the next thing that the text teaches is the purpose He has for us. Again, the evidence that we produce fruit; the purpose is to produce fruit. There should be some evidence that He is in our lives by the fruit we produce, the fact that we are doing it is part of our purpose. We are to produce fruit. Matthew 28: 19—20 reads, "[19] Therefore go and make disciples of all nations, baptizing them in the name of the Father and of the Son and of the Holy Spirit, [20] and teaching them to obey everything I have commanded you. And surely I am with you always, to the very end of the age." Well right there, He is telling us that we are to do the things that He has done and modeled for us here on Earth. He is a great teacher; He modeled for us the excellence that He expects and it is as simple as that. It doesn't get any simpler than I did it for you and I need you to do it for Me through others. That is it, it doesn't get any simpler than that.

We have to ask ourselves: "Are we living out His purpose for us?" As I mentioned that I have authored 32 books so far, and when I asked the Lord, "What do You want me to do when You give me another book?" He titled it, He outlined it, He allowed it to progress from outline to discussion to writing it, to be able to get to print, and to get into bookstores and internationally distributed and to get the book online; He allowed the whole process to happen. I had to let my guard down to let myself be clear that this is part of my purpose.

There are things that are part of your purpose that you are not handling. You are not handling some of your responsibilities well; you are actually ignoring them. You are hoping the responsibilities will go away. You are simply questioning God and asking Jesus, "Why have You just let me be gifted in this manner, now I am held accountable for this?" Do you think that anybody just wants to be a teacher when the Bible says that teachers will be held more accountable than anybody else? Does that then mean preachers? Does that mean deacons? In

God's ominous voice, He speaks and says, "It says teachers ma'am, get it straight! It says teachers and I have called you into the gift of teaching so what I need you to do, regardless of how you think about it know that you will be held accountable for teaching and that if you are not teaching does not mean you are held any less accountable."

'Well how can you be held accountable when you are not teaching?' It is because you have a gift of teaching and you should be teaching, so if you are not teaching and you ignore your gifts, you are accountable for that as well. We got to keep in mind that God has come to do certain things. He has plans and the plans He has for your life are sometimes intimately related to the plans He has for my life, so we have to make sure that we are clear about how to make that happen for ourselves? The purpose He has for you or on purpose, in fact in Jeremiah 29:11 God says, "I know the plans that I have for you," says the Lord. The purpose and the plans go together; He has plans based on the purpose. What do I want her to do? What do I want her to be? The plans are related to that. In my case, because God wanted me to be an author, so He gave me the gift of writing. God wanted me to teach and preach, He gave me the gift of teaching. God gave it to me so that I can carry out His purpose. It was not meant for me to carry out my own selfish purposes. It was designed for me to carry out the things that are of You, things that You made for me to use those gifts to accomplish. You gave me those gifts God because of what You planned for me to have and planned for me to do and who You planned for me to minister to, and those people are all already ordained.

POWER

The third thing is that He gives is power. Now understand that we have that power and that power comes from God. I often hear, 'Well I have my own power.' I understand that you think that have your own power, your own strength. What I do not get and what I do not understand is you thinking that it comes from you, that you self-generated that power. You self-generated that power? But it is not from you! You did not create that power by yourself. You are not responsible for that by yourself. You cannot infuse that power in yourself. Everything that you have comes from God! Everything we have comes from God! Col. 1: 10 – 12 says [10] so that you may live a life worthy of the Lord and please Him in every way: bearing fruit in every good work, growing in the knowledge of God, [11] being strengthened with all power according to His glorious might so that you may have great endurance and patience, [12] and giving joyful thanks to the Father, who has qualified you to share in the inheritance of His holy people in the kingdom of light.

We have access to power but it is not our power. It is given to you to use to bring God glory. That is why you have power. Not to self-edify. Not to be self-serving. Not to just be simply selfish, but to serve the Father. When you consider 'why do I have this power, why do I think I am powerful, why has He given me this sphere of influence, why has God done these things?' It is because you need to use that power and that influence for His kingdom, for His glory, and to uplift His servants and others around Him that He wants to become His servants. He gives you that because of the sphere of influence that you already placed you there. He uses that even more and to give it to you for the building of His kingdom, ultimately, that is it. God's power outweighs ours. We will never be more powerful than God. He won't allow us to be more powerful than Him. We cannot be stronger than God; we cannot be more anything than God! Why? Because we are His creations and we are not smarter than the Creator. We are not stronger than the Creator.

So understand for yourself that there should be some evidence, that power should be evidence. 2Timothy 1:7 (NASB) reads, [7] For God has not given us a spirit of timidity, but of power and love and discipline. So that is to say, He gave us the power that we have, and we treat it as such. It is a privilege; it is an honor. We treat it special because we are His children and no other reason. There should be some evidence that you are a child of God. There should be some evidence that the Lord has taken over your life. You shouldn't have point that out to anyone that 'I am not what I used to be, and I am not where I ought to be.' You do not have to tell anybody that because that already is true. It is already true that you are different, it is already true. As a result of that being already true, it is already true for all of us. He has given us the gifts, and He has given us the power to carry on and use them to build His kingdom.

He has already given us those things, so why is it that we act as if we do not know. We act as if we do not know that He is present in our lives. We act as if we do not know that He has a purpose for our lives. Up to a certain point we are living that purpose out, but there are times we get beside ourselves, and act the there is no power within us.

Paul speaks to the church at Ephesus, to the Ephesians, in chapter 3 verses 14 – 21, and some of my favorite scriptures. Verse 16 reads, "I pray that out of His glorious riches He may strengthen you with power through His Spirit in your inner being." Not giving you physical brute strength but power and strength in your inner being: strength in your soul, in your spirit, in your mind, and in your heart; that you are powerful in areas where people cannot touch. That is the kind of power we have to overcome odds through faith, the way He designed; power to take care of the things He has assigned, for each and every one of us. That is the type of power that we are looking for, that He has given us.

So there should be some evidence of God in your life. There should be some evidence that you have done some things on His behalf whether people know about them or not. It is such power that empowers us that others would want to know where that power comes from. It will be naturally oozing without you having to give it any assistance; it can stand on its own, it doesn't need any help. There should be some evidence through your talk, through your walk, through your actions, through your growth, through the things that you want to say; there should be some evidence.

Amen.

Lord God, how we bless You and love You and thank You this day. I thank You Lord God right now because You have done inside of us so many beautiful and wonderful things. So Lord, I thank You right now for blessing us with the earth, at a profound and unprecedented level. Lord, we thank You so much that You are just God and God alone. I thank You for this message that went forth today, I thank You right now that You allowed me to do exactly what You wanted me to do and I appreciate You using me to do so. Lord, thank You right now that You are just God and God alone. So Lord, I thank You right now for what You have done and what You are going to do; for forgiving us of our sins and we are able to take this message and share with others about there should be some evidence and what these evidence looks like in our lives. Amen.

Love Without Hypocrisy
Exodus 34:5-7 (NIV)

⁵ Then the LORD came down in the cloud and stood there with him and proclaimed His name, the LORD. ⁶ And He passed in front of Moses, proclaiming, "The LORD, the LORD, the compassionate and gracious God, slow to anger, abounding in love and faithfulness, ⁷ maintaining love to thousands, and forgiving wickedness, rebellion and sin. Yet He does not leave the guilty unpunished; He punishes the children and their children for the sin of the parents to the third and fourth generation."

Exodus 34:5-7 (NIV)

Lord God, how we thank You and we love You this day. How we hope that You will consider us, how You are worthy of our praise and our glory, so Lord God we thank You right now for what You will say to us today. For what You will share with us in our time together today. So, Lord God I thank You right now, for love without hypocrisy. Thank You for using me to do what You will and I thank You for forgiving me of my sins. Thank You for hiding me behind Your cross and allowing me to do what is pleasing in thy sight. In Jesus name, I pray Amen.

GOD'S INTENTIONAL DEFINITION OF LOVE

Love without hypocrisy. When you consider the definition of love. The first milestone is that love is unconditional and love is without consequence, love is not to be repaid, and some other things that we always want to remind ourselves of. The hardest part of all of that is remembering that as we define love, God is the very definition of that love and we have to ask ourselves are we doing exactly what we are supposed to be doing in regard to that definition. Are we doing exactly what we are supposed to be doing in reference to the definition? Are we doing those things, because if we are doing those things, then how is it that we have to struggle with loving each other.

When we look at our scripture text, verse six, And He passed in front of Moses, proclaiming, "The LORD, the LORD, the compassionate and gracious God, slow to anger, abounding in love and faithfulness. And abounding in love means there's no limit to what His love will do, who it will cover, and how long it will last. There is no limit to what it is He's giving to each of us, there is no limit to His graciousness. We consider what God wants from us regarding love. Are we there? Are we falling short? How is it that we can function in this situation, understanding what His definition of love is and are we really living to that definition of love?

So, hypocrisy, hypocrites, hypocritical. As we consider those words in definition form, it means someone who says they are something, but they are definitely not. Well, what do you mean by that? Well I'm pretty clear, that if you do not, if you're not who you say you are, if you're not representing yourself as you said, who you said you were, that is definitely a hypocritical situation. You are saying that you are a loving person, but nothing that you do says love. If saying that you are a loving person, then nothing you did speaks love. Your actions, your words, your deeds, your tone, none of those things speak love. And hypocritical means I say I love you, but I do not do anything that is like love.

I think that people find it difficult to love others because they do not love themselves. The Lord says love thy neighbor as thyself, well that is a problem right there. People do not love themselves enough to love somebody else, so you cannot be mad when they do not love you because they do not love themselves. So that is not a point of contention, it is a point of understanding you know that love is not as evident and as profound or as available as one might think.

So, and finally I want to define the Lord. When He puts these scriptures together, verse 5 reads, Then the LORD came down in the cloud and stood there with him and proclaimed His name, the LORD. You are the Entity, the Deity, the Person, the Spirit, the Everything and You created the everything. And inside of Your Lordship, You are the only Object, Person, Entity, Spirit, and the only Entity that can define Yourself. We cannot define the Lord for Him. We cannot define the Lord for others. He defines Himself for each of us so we can just share that information with others.

Similar to the rule in English which says you cannot use a word to define that same word, and while that is true, I just have a huge, huge thing about being able to say, the Lord. He has made it so very clear on how we are to interact with Him. You see while He is communicating with Moses, He's sharing with Moses, He's trying to teach Moses, He's trying to allow Moses to understand, He comes to Moses as clouds. Now this is the scene where Moses is chiseling the two stone tablets like the first ones, because he broke the first set of tablets right? But the Lord is giving you an opportunity to get two other tablets and try this again.

Now these stone tablets are very important. These aren't just your run of the mill tablets, these are tablets that were blessed by God. That were shared with Moses directly from God and verse chapter 34, the Lord said to Moses, 'Chisel out two stone tablets like the first ones and I will write on them the words that were on the first ones which you broke.' The Lord wrote on these tablets Himself. And you let them break? The love part comes in when God says, 'I'm going to do this again for you. I've already done this one time, I'm going to do it one more time for you.' Because the rest of us would have just been upset. You broke my _____, and you go right down to the Target, Wal-Mart, Piggly Wiggly, Nordstrom, Marshall Field's, Macy's or wherever and buy another vase. You broke this vase, so now I'm upset with you to the point where I cannot speak to you because you broke a vase. A replaceable material item, a vase.

We are talking about some stone tablets that have on it the law, handwritten by God Himself. The Lord and you broke them and He's still not angry. That is the Lord our God, that is how He can define Himself within Himself by Himself because those are the types of activities that He makes and does.

First, He tells him to be ready in the morning, then come up on Mt. Sinai, present yourself to Me there on top of the mountain. "No one is to come with you or be seen anywhere on the mountain, not even flocks and herds may graze in front of the mountain, ok?" We are dealing with a forgiving God, a loving God. ⁵ Then the LORD came down in the cloud and stood there with him and proclaimed His name, the LORD. ⁶ And He passed in front of Moses, proclaiming, "The LORD, the LORD, the compassionate and gracious God, slow to anger, abounding in love and faithfulness, ⁷ maintaining love to thousands, and forgiving wickedness, rebellion and sin.

GOD'S ISNESS

We will examine is—who He is. When God defines Hhimself, and all that needs to be is Is, one word that defines, and it is Is. The Is is in and of itself enough because He is.

There's a song that we sang recently at church but it was something I've known since I was a small girl, a very new Christian, and it is God Is; that is the name of the song 'God Is.' And the words go something like this: 'God is. God is the joy and the strength of my life. He moves all pain misery and strife. God is. God is, oh yes He is, God is my all and all.' So when you talk about God is, His isness. the form of is comes from the word of being, and when we talk about being and being intimate and being Him and Is, just in His presence Is, and who He Is. His isness is enough to understand that His love is without hypocrisy. God is not going to love you today and quit loving you tomorrow. It is not possible. It is not what He does. It is not going to happen.

In that likeness that we are supposed to be like God, that is what we are to do. Now a problem that we have is that we cannot do it because we have something else. We have something else interrupting that isness. We have something that interrupts that isness. We have got ourselves, our sin, our transgressions that interrupt that isness and we cannot get to a point where we cannot get from beside ourselves. And so in that, His isness, His Is is intentional.

GOD'S INTENTIONAL LOVE

Watch how God addresses Moses in verse one. God says, 'Since you did this, since you broke them, now I have to give you another pair. Come back where we were, let's start again and I'm going to give them to you. I'm going to give them to you again.' His love is intentional. His love is very intentional because of the things that He does. He starts that process all over again. And He says, 'I want you to come and do this again.' He intends to be compassionate. He lets you know that upfront. He intends to fulfill His very promises. He does that on purpose. He tells us that. He wants us to be sure that we are clear. He wants to be sure that we are aware of what exactly He is doing. He wants to be sure that we are aware completely and fully about what it is He wants us to do. It is intentional.

It is also intentional that God wants us to do this as well. IT is no misunderstanding what He wants us to do. It is no misunderstanding about what He has designed for us to do. He tells Moses very specific instructions. He plans for us to follow those. He gives Moses step by step instructions about what to do. And when He does those things he wants Moses to follow exactly what it is He said. He defines love in an intentional fashion.

Fast forward several thousands years and look at what He did when He gave us Christ. John 3:16 says in a very familiar passage, for God so loved the world. Let's look at that very small word: so. Because He loved us so much, which is very much lined up with His abounding love, slow to anger, compassionate and graciousness, gracious God. Maintaining love for thousands. Can you give visual to how it is that He can abound in love. Giving love to thousands. Forgiving wickedness, rebellion and sin. That is love.

Some people cannot forgive their own children. And they birthed them. And for years and you were not the maker or creator or anything; you were just a vessel to get here and you were my transportation, if you will. Yet, you determine when you can and cannot love me, when you will and will not love me, and when you will do and you won't do. And we do that intentionally. We intentionally do not love the other person like we should. We do it intentionally. We set out to do that. That is just too much. The fact that you made that happen, is too much. Ask yourself when you decide to make those decisions about when you are going to intentionally, and unintentionally love somebody, what are you saying? What are you saying to God?

While that may seem shallow or while that may not seem deep enough, look at what you have done. Jesus commands that we love one another. That was a command. He says in Ephesians five, love your wife as Christ loved church, Ephesians chapter four, verse 32, be kind and compassionate to one another, loving and forgiving one another. It is woven through the fabric of the Bible, thus our Christianity, thus our rules, in Exodus, earlier in this same chapter, He told him that you were supposed to love in Exodus 20. And you tell me that it is optional to love. Optional? We act as if love is optional, then what we are saying is that we are not following His laws, His decrees, His commands, we are not being obedient. It says if we love Him, then we are to obey what He commands.

So how many different ways do you think we can avoid the obedience that we are designed to demonstrate and we are told to exhibit, and then still get what it is we have asked for and be able to appreciate what we are supposed to be as the Christians that He's called us to be? Well, we say we want to be closer to God that means we have got to do some things like put those things aside, put that hate aside, put that anti love aside, put those things aside. Put it aside. We have got to put it aside. Forgive ourselves and forgive others and keep focused on His plan.

Now, we talked about His Isness, His Is, He is love. He is the very definition of love, He is the creator and author and finisher of love. He is the perfector of love, He is the ultimate in how love is defined and carried out, practiced daily, maintained, managed and monitored.

One of the things I do as I help couples in counseling; I help couples become better married couples. One of the things I ask them is have you equipped your mate to love you. And they often laugh yes I did, I told her everything, I let her know this I told her that, I did not keep any secrets, blah blah blah blah blah. I counter with, 'well what about this?' No, well then you did not do it. God gives us everything we need to love him, to love ourselves and to love others. That is the entirety of His command to love him.

Deuteronomy chapter 6, verse 5 says, 'Love the LORD your God with all your heart and with all your soul and with all your strength.' That is the total makeup of who you are. There's no way around that. The verse starts with love the Lord your God. Verse five through nine says, ⁵ Love the LORD your God with all your heart and with all your soul and with all your strength. ⁶ These commandments that I give you today are to be on your hearts. ⁷ Impress them on your children. Talk about them when you sit at home and when you walk along the road, when you lie down and when you get up. ⁸ Tie them as symbols on your hands and bind them on your foreheads. ⁹ Write them on the doorframes of your houses and on your gates.

So, understand that you are to love the Lord your God. You love Him. You love Him? But what you're doing does not show or exhibit that love. It doesn't show or exhibit that love at all. We are to have evidence; there should be some evidence of our love to God. And when there's not any evidence, then basically we are saying, it is optional. However, it is not at all optional.

GOD'S INTENSE LOVE

So, His love, the love of which He is the intentional definition, His intentional loving of us, He is intentional, and now I want to talk about the intensity. How He loves us. God is very intense. If there is any doubt about that, let's look at some of the things that He has done. When we upset Him and when we have excited Him and made Him happy. Look at the intensity. Look at the lengths He has gone, He formed us out of the dust, and created us and blew into us the breath of life. Then He put him to sleep, and God took out his rib and now your bones are my bones and you are flesh of my flesh. He made a woman so that the man could have a companion.

God's very detailed and He's very intense. God made a man, out of nothing. Some dust. God made a woman out of his rib. God did not actually need his rib to make this woman. God could have made her likewise out of dust, but there was a partnership that God formed and a relationship He was very intentional about and God was very intense about His Creations. Now, God could have made Jesus out of that very same dust. God could have taken the rib out of someone and made Jesus. God could have made Jesus from dust. God could have made Jesus appear, but God put Jesus inside of a virgin girl. There's an intensity there. And God foretold Jesus' arrival several thousand years before. And so with that, God has been intense about His strategy regarding love, He has been exceptionally profound in the ways that He has handle me and loving me. What about you?

And God's intensity to us. He loves us when we do not love ourselves. He loves us when we doubt His love for us. He loves us regardless of what it is we have done and what we are going to do. He knows that we are going to mess up. He is well aware that we are about to make a mess, He loves us anyway.

Ephesians two verses nine through ten, is often quoted, familiar scriptures, reads: [8] For it is by grace you have been saved, through faith—and this is not from yourselves, it is the gift of God— [9] not by works, so that no one can boast. Now I do not know about you, but that is a very evidence of intense love. Knowing me before You knitted me in my mother's womb, Jeremiah chapter one, verse five, that is evidence of an intense love. Jeremiah 29:11, that is evidence, for You know the plans You have for me, plans to provide me with a future and a peace and not to harm me, that is an intense love. We walk around every day knowing that there are people out to harm us, they intend to harm us, they told us first, initially, and up front, 'I am going to harm you.' It is something I plan to do, and something I'm looking forward to, I'm planning it right now, to harm you.

We should ask ourselves. How can we better understand, what we are assigned to, how can we better love others with a God-type love. How can we better live the commands that we have been so repeatedly forgiven for not carrying out and intentionally overlooking avoiding, averting our eyes toward, acting as if we have never heard or seen those commands before. Reminding ourselves that we too need love, we do not want to give it out not because we just do not want to do the right thing on purpose. We don't think that we can afford to love another person.

I posted on social media recently about being able to find love and measure that, to develop the definition. One of the responses received was love out loud, daily, and on purpose. And the author of it really meant live. Live it out day to day and I just love how the author messed up, but meant so much more. Hillary Weeks has a song that says if I only had today. And if you only had today, how would you manage your love, your measure of love, your definition of love, your isness in your love, your intensity, and your intentional love? How would that be measured up to God's measuring tool and how would you change what it is you're doing if you are not? I ask myself that all the time, 'are you the very walking, talking, working definition of love?' Are you that person? Because at the end of every day, at the end of every hour, at the end of every moment, you were designed to love, you were created to love. You were developed out of love because He loved you first.

My children came home from vacation bible school one year and they said, 'we learned the song Jesus loved me this I know for the Bible tells me so.' I said, 'Is that all you learned?' They said, 'no.' I said, 'but that was enough.' Knowing that He loves you regardless intimately, not figuratively or parenthetically, or theoretically. He loves us unconditionally and He loves you right now every day of all the seconds of our lives. Barring nothing that you have done. If we can get that around our mind and our spirit because somehow we have avoided that, we have walked away, we have intimately figured out how to divorce ourselves from the concept of God's love and we have to stop that because that is not the God we serve. That is not what we do.

His love without hypocrisy is powerful to lift your head, heart, and spirit. His definition is everlasting. His intentions will never be questioned. His isness will never be revoked. His intensity can never be replaced or negotiated.

His love! We need it—can't get along without it; even when we appear to reject it.

He loves me and there's nothing I can do to undo it.

Amen.

The Lord how we bless You and how we love You. We thank You for loving us. We thank You for the isness of your love. For the beauty of the intensity of Your love, we thank You for the intentionalness of your love. We just thank You right now Lord God that You love us and love us unconditionally. We ask You to forgive us of our sins. We thank You right now for blessing us just as we are. Thank You for the plans You have for us and thank You for the anointing placed on our lives. Thank You for our gifts and thank You for having somewhere to serve and use those gifts. Thank You for this word that went forward today, allow it to bless and provide to those who will hear it and then those who will share it. Thank You for the messenger on this day, Lord God, that she may do exactly what You called on her to do every single day and that she learns to love better and more intentionally and more intensely as well Lord God. We thank You right now. It is in Your Son's, Jesus' name that we pray and ask these blessings. Amen.

Anger is Real and Does Not Have to Cost
Ephesians 4:26-27

[26] "In your anger do not sin": Do not let the sun go down while you are still angry, [27] and do not give the devil a foothold.

Ephesians 4:26-27 NIV

[26] Be ye angry, and sin not: let not the sun go down upon your wrath:

[27] Neither give place to the devil.

Ephesians 4:26-27 KJV

Lord God, I cannot thank You enough for this message, this word. Lord, thank You for letting me be Your preach today. I thank You for allowing it to happen in Your time. And I thank You right now for what is about to transpire here for today and just allow me to just speak what it is You would have for me to say today. Lord God, it is in Jesus' name, I pray this prayer. Amen.

Our sermon title is Anger is Real and Doesn't Have to Cost. First of all, I want to talk about the title for a moment. Anger is real. It is not a situation at all where anger is something that is not real. It is not something that we want to deal with, but anger is real. It is a real emotion. It is something that many of us have experienced before. Everyone has experienced anger. Even Jesus has been angry in the Bible.

We do not want to ever be confused about that emotion and say it to someone, 'you shouldn't be angry. You're a Christian.' That is not what the word of God says. Acknowledges that anger is okay. It is a natural response. The scripture teaches us that while it is okay to be angry, it is not okay to sin because of your anger. Your anger can not cause you to sin.

Your anger should not be used as an excuse for you to sin. It should not be a scenario where you think that because I'm angry then I can do everything that I want. That is not the situation. When we are angry, we need to use that anger for something useful. Use that energy for something useful. Avoid what we normally do.

Let me tell you how the scriptures became some of my favorite scriptures. I have a very passionate personality. Whatever I'm into I'm very passionate about that. If it is my writing, I'm very passionate about my writing. When it is my preaching, I'm very passionate about my preaching. When it is teaching, I'm very passionate about teaching. I am very passionate about those things that are within my reach, that are within my grasp, that are within my favorite things.

And so likewise, that height of emotion, I'm also very passionate about things that mean something to me, people that mean something to me. And so there have been times when there are things that have happened that have angered me in such a fashion where I have had to say, I am just really angry and I need to take some time. But I had this thing where if I got angry, then I wanted to react and respond.

And so in order to not react or to respond, especially something that I couldn't take back or that I was going to regret, I had to put myself in the position where in the point of my anger I had to learn not to sin. See one of those things that happens to us if we were angry, if we were emotional, we are upset, when we feel bad, certain things take place. I call it your 'go-to,' your 'go-to' cannot be something where sin is going to resort. Your 'go-to' cannot be defined as sin. These scriptures keep me from my sinful 'go-to's.'

There's a rule in the NFL that says the ground cannot cause a fumble. What that means that when you have the ball tucked under your arm, you had control of the ball when you hit the ground. If the impact of your body against the ground caused the ball to come out of your grasp, the rule on the field is that the ball is dead, and the play is over. Whatever forward progress you made, that is where the ball would be set. But it is not going to be a fumble if you had complete control of the ball when you fall. Similar to this, you have complete control of who you are and your emotions. When you do not have complete control of that and when it causes you to sin, you need to ask God for some help.

So, let's understand that Jesus' anger was expressed. He turned over a table. Whoo!!! Jesus turned over a table, in His expression of His anger. Because we have made His Father's house a den of thieves because they were using that area in the sanctuary to sell their wares and pilfer goods and whatever. We cannot get so angry that we want to sin, or we actually sin. Did Jesus hurt somebody? Quite possibly. Could Jesus have cast them down or killed them? He could've done a lot of things, but Jesus had to be Jesus and He cannot sin. He expressed how He felt. He corrected their behavior and then He had to go and calm down. No more actions did He take.

Likewise, we need to get into a position where we say, 'that upset me, but I'm not going to my 'go-to.' Wherever the 'go-to' is, I'm not going to my 'go-to.' I'm not going to resort to shopping or drinking or staying out late. I'm not going to resort to any of those things.'

So, anger is okay; it is a natural response. However, sin that is a result of that anger is not okay. It is not a solution. Your anger can not be solutioned by sins. Sin is not going to cause the behavior that got you angry to change. We want to put a band aid on something for which we really need to find the solution. The solution to your anger is going to have to be solved with whatever the situation was. So that means communication about the fact that this is not okay. We need to change this. We need to figure this out differently. Communication is a solution to your anger.

When we consider what does it take to make us angry, we probably want to also modify that. But how do you modify what makes you angry? Well, there are certain things you just decide are not going to make me angry. The scripture reads be ye transformed by the renewing of your mind. Part of what happened when your mind is renewed is the same things that anger you are not going to anger you anymore. The same thing that caused you trouble is not going to continue to cause you trouble anymore.

When you think over the things that get you upset, as you renew your mind and become a new creature in Christ, those things should not still be happening. Romans chapter 12, verses 1 and 2 reads, "Therefore, I urge you, brothers and sisters, in view of God's mercy, to offer your bodies as a living sacrifice, holy and pleasing to God—this is your true and proper worship. [2] Do not conform to the pattern of this world, but be transformed by the renewing of your mind. Then you will be able to test and approve what God's will is—His good, pleasing and perfect will."

This relationship between angry and transformation: It is then when you renew your mind, the same things that caused you to be angry are not going to be able to cause you to be angry anymore. You're not going to want to get upset about all the same little things you previously did because you have grown spiritually, you have matured, you want to change what bothers you. For six months, maybe a year, that was my scripture. When it looked like I was going to be angry, I said those scriptures. "In your anger, do not sin and do not let the sun falling in your wrath. Do not let the devil a foothold."

And I would easily calm down and think, 'okay is it that big of a deal? How can this be solved and resolved? And what would I need to do to fix it?' Well, with that in mind, I just proceeded to fix it, not resorting to the 'go-to,' not doing something I would later regret and have to ask for forgiveness for, none of that. I said my scriptures and then I was able to move on. Well, finally there was a point in which I did not need to say those scriptures to take action. I just thought of the behavior.

Just solve it. Is it a big deal? How are we going to resolve it? How can it be fixed? And then, people started looking and reacting differently because they thought, 'oh, she's going to be angry. Oh, she was going to be upset.' Well now, technically, we do not know if she's angry or not. All we know is that she's solving it. She's communicating with us. It is being resolved. It is no longer an issue. We weren't expecting that.

The things that other people did which they thought would ignite my anger, and caused me to sin or caused me to get upset, and they got ready for 'table flipping,' that no longer happened. They had to change up how they handled trying to do those things to me. Or they handled me differently because, hey you know, we cannot get her upset like we used to. What we are going to do? We cannot get her all riled up. What we are going to do?

Ask yourself, are people pushing your buttons on purpose to see the show and that you can really give them that show that they're trying to stand as audience for? With that in question, we must manage ourselves differently and anger is a part of who you are. Your response is also very intricate part of you. It is very critical that you respond in a good manner. Anger has to be managed in a better method than we previously have.

Now, anger should be ended quickly. The scripture says: in your anger, do not sin. And do not let the sun fall on your wrath. Do not let the sun go down while you're still angry. Well, I live in Texas. We honor day light savings time. At certain parts of the year, it is dark at 6 o'clock. So if I'll get angry at 5:30, I got about 30 minutes to get that together. Do not let the sun fall while you're still angry. Do not let the sun go down while you're still angry.

By sheer observation the sun is going to rise and set everyday as long as God says so. But if it doesn't, it is not based on your anger. The sun is not going to stay in the air in over the atmosphere because you are angry. So technically that means you are the person who has to relinquish the anger and the sun is going to go down regardless. Here's why that is important. You hear a couple say, 'do not go to bed angry.' And the purpose of that has been, or you will never know if a person will wake up, if that is the last thing you said to that person. There is regret when you are angry when they died.

And while part of that is true, technically, it is something that we could use here as an example. Keep in mind that there are other things that have to happen in the evening. And why you want to let that anger propel and perpetuated that far and that long. We do not want our anger to go on so long that it becomes a part of us. When we were not able to shovel off anger quickly, it becomes embedded in you. Once you have to still talk about that anger over and over and over again, it becomes a part of who you are. Then you do not know why you're angry because you forgot because you're just focused on being angry.

'I'm not going to let it go. I'm going to hold a grudge.' Well, you know what, that impedes your blessings not the person with whom you are angry. Being angry beyond that period of time is going to cancel some things God had in store for you. By not being angry when the sun goes down, you do not take them into tomorrow. Do not take your past into right now. It is not worth it. Is it really, do you want to really just to be angry? You want to spend your emotional time being angry? You want to spend the time that has given to you blessed by God or designated for you to do certain things to be spent being angry?

I will tell you beyond a shadow of a doubt, you have been shortening your years definitively by staying angry. And I also want to remind you that the person that you're angry with is going on to do other things. And they're not worried about you being angry. I do not care if that person sleeps with you at night or sleeps in the home where you are or somebody at work or somebody at the grocery store, or in the parking lot, they have gone on with their lives. They do not care that you're angry. They do not care.

The only person who's concerned about you being angry is you. And you're blocking all kinds of blessings, cancelling all kinds of love and not being able to share the experience because you are angry. And now, you cannot even remember what you're angry about. So you got to get in the position where the sun goes down at 6 o'clock, you're not supposed to even be angry at that time. Let it go. How can we solve this? How can we get this resolved? How can we finish our day out strong and positive if we just let this anger go now? What was really making us angry about this whole situation?

Cannot we just find resolve and be resolved? That was the question that we need to ask ourselves. Literally, what do we need to know. That is all that we need to know. So I'm just saying that when we get to that point of asking ourselves how can I be done with this anger and not take this into the evening or the next day. You got to spend time on that. You got to get that figured out where you can sustain your life. And put it in a fashion where anger is not something that you focus on.

How can I focus on something other than being angry? How can I move ahead without being angry? Can I disband anger from my routine? How can I show others that being angry is not what I focused on anymore and you cannot easily anger me the same way you used to be able to so please stop doing that, this and the other and understand who I am in my new self, in my renewed mind, in my refreshed spirit because I'm not going to harbor that?

If you're angry with someone, you're not even supposed to give an offering to God. It says, put your offering on the altar and then go back and make peace, make the forgiveness, make nice if you will, use some colloquial terms with your neighbor and then bring our offering to the Lord so He will accept it. We do not do that. We put our offering in the tray and keep moving. Is that really what we are supposed to do? The answer to that is no.

So we got to keep our mindset on the fact that anger is okay. But it is not something we want to sin because of. We want to find the quickest solution to being angry and we definitely do not want to take this in beyond something that so that we do not take that into tomorrow. We have got to quit figuring out how to harbor anger. Who has time to store that anger? Where do you put that energy? I do not hold a grudge very well. I really do not.

There are people who think I'm angry with them and I'm not. As a matter of fact, it takes a whole lot to even remember what I was upset about. Now, technically does that mean I actually forgave them—I have to investigate that on a case by case basis but if I remember what I was upset about, forgiveness has not happened. I have a great memory but God does not let me hold on to that. I can remember things from when I was three and four and five years old. However, He does no let me tell you some things on why I'm angry with you or why I was angry with you or why I'm upset about something.

He does not allow for that. I do not have the time and the place for that in my life because I have to do so many other things, I cannot do that. Understand that anger is one of those things you have to manage because you're the only person who can manage it well. And I will promise you that I do not really think you want God to manage your anger. I do not think you want God to manage the anger that you have. You do not want Him to manage that.

I am no expert but I have this feeling it would be my suspicion that when He handles that anger, He's going to definitely help you manage it in the fashion that He's going to be pleased about. I can tell that God has a wrath but His will, will be done. And if He has to use His override button to get His will done, you certainly won't get to be angry as often as you previously had if ever in the future. And you'll wonder why am I responding this way? And why are people concerned and consumed with my renewed response as I am?

That is not a technique I will want to employ. So we deal with anger issue quickly. Anger should definitely not be taken into tomorrow. It should not be harbored. It really should not be held. Jesus preached about forgiveness. He teaches on 70 times 7. Some of us have done the math already. That is 490 times. That is for the same person. It doesn't matter if it is the same offense or a different offense, you have to forgive them. And if you had time to count the 490, we are going to give you something new to do.

Because I got to tell you that metaphorically, 490 means an infinite amount of time and keeping count is not something we do or operating in the love that Christ said as we should share which is shared in 1 Corinthians 13, that love does not keep count of wrong. We need to love our neighbors as ourselves. We cannot keep counting their wrongs and metaphorically, that 490 means that it is an infinite amount of time you're going to forgive them over and over again. And it is going to be okay that you forgive them over and over again.

DO NOT GIVE THE DEVIL OR THOSE HE IS USING TOOLS FOR ADVANCEMENT

Do not give the devil or those he is using any tools for advancement. Do not give the devil or those he is using any tools for advancement. This is by far my favorite point. The text reads, and do not give the devil a foothold. Do not give the devil a foothold. Well, what that means is that we are not going to give the devil a place to take root. We do not want to give the devil a place to get comfortable.

If the devil knows that he can change who you are, persuade you over to his side, gives you reason to disband and abandon all of the learnings and teachings that you know about the Lord behind the behavior that you're going to have by anger, then the devil has a foothold. If the devil can plant in your mind, 'you should be angry with her or you should hold that grudge to Jesus comes back, it'll be okay.' That is not what we are designed to do by no stretch of the imagination. You do not give the devil any further source to plant his foolishness for you. You just do not. It is not something you do.

'Well, they did _____.' I understand that. I do. And he hurt me, I totally get it. I understand he totally disrespected, she totally disrespected you. I get it. But what I also need you to get is that in all of that, nothing happened to you. God is still your God. He is still able to forgive. He is still able to heal. He is still able to comfort. He is still able to stand there in your place. He is still there. He also left you Jesus and the Holy Spirit. So you have all this whole team of people, God, Jesus, and the Holy Spirit, that help you with how you feel, what you think, and what you want.

They have not abandoned you. They have not left you. They are still right there while this other person has misused you and abused you and all. They're still right there. They have not gone anywhere, nowhere. So understand that giving the devil a foothold is going to undermine the plans that He has set forth for you because you want to give time away, precious, valuable time when you should be serving God by giving the devil an audience. We do not give the devil an audience. That is out, no brainer, not going to be able to do it, not happening, not even close to the right answer.'

What we need to understand is you give the devil an audience when you're angry too long. You take that anger too intensely. You take that anger too far. I mean you indulge in it. You respond to it. You do some things you regret later. You say some words you cannot take back. You hurt more intentionally and more intensely than the person hurt you and then you find out they did not intend to hurt you at all. But you said some things, you have done some things you cannot take it back. Your anger can not put you in that position where you are postured in a no-win situation.

And while God can do all things, you severed some things such that He's got to do some real repair in order to get their heart back in a same arena as yours, so you all could be in a relationship with Him again. All the while, everything else around you is on pause because you cannot get further than right there. It was not designed to do that. Sometimes we are presented some issues that are designed to anger us to see if we were mature enough to get passed that point. If we spend too long there, that devil is going to get a foothold.

He's going to stir the pot, if you will. He's going to take that anger. He's going to use it to keep you angry, to distance you from others, to keep you captive in your own mind. When he does those things, he's won. You have given him the audience he's asked for. That is not okay. When we hold grudges because we are angry, because something happened that already has evolved and over with, then done for several years now, we take the power and we try to transfer to somebody else. Now it is still God's power, but you're ignoring that now. You have decided 'I'm not going to do that; I'm not just going to let it go. I do not need to do that. Why would I let it go?' Because He said to.

So I said do not give the devil a foothold, or those he is using any tools for advancement. The devil has an agenda. The devil asked Jesus to sift Peter. Jesus said, "I'm praying for you." The devil asked for access to Job and Lord says I trust him. You can do everything to him, but you cannot harm him. The devil is allowed to access you only by the consent and permission and the perfect will of God. So we got to ask ourselves and remind ourselves that this is happening under His direct supervision so He is watching my response and my behavior. He is right here. He is not missing. God knows exactly what's happening.

Now, understand the devil is not going to show up as this charismatic character with this pitch fork with the red suit on and his horns that we made him up to be, rather he shows up in people. And I call those people he is using and anybody who sides with the devil satan as well. They can be the devil for a few days, some hours, for a few minutes, this lifetime, whatever. They can play the part, but do not give them room for advancement by your behaviors, by your lack of response of positivity. Do not do that.

Amen.

Lord God, I thank You right now for this messages worth. Thank You for the heart and minds that it will touch. Thank You for the spirit that it will move. And Lord God, thank You for what You have done for me. Thank You for reminding me of who You are in my life and why You're the most prominent person, the most special thing, the most human being in my whole existence life and thank You for our relationship. And I thank You right now for the gift and call on my life. Thank You for this time we have had to share. And I ask You to forgive me of my sins and those of us who are also listening to this our message

Lord. I thank You right now for this message, its contents, and its reach. And I thank You for its portability. In Jesus name, we pray and ask these blessings. Amen.

Do You Hear the Words Coming Out of My Mouth
Ephesians 4:29

²⁹ Do not let any unwholesome talk come out of your mouths, but only what is helpful for building others up according to their needs, that it may benefit those who listen.

Ephesians 4:29 (NIV)

Oh God, we thank You right now for Your love, grace, mercy, sovereignty, forgiveness and Your guided love, we thank You right now Lord God for the provisions You make for each of us, thank You for covering us with our portion of health, strength and will. Thank You lord God for blessing our finances, our families, and our futures. Lord God, we thank You right now for this time of study and Lord God if You will let the meditations in my heart and what comes out of my mouth is pleasing in your sight Thank You right now for those who hear this lesson, this message, may it anoint and bless them in a special way. Lord God, I thank You right now for all You have done for me, and how this word has blessed me in the process. Thank You very much in Your Son, Jesus' name we pray. Amen.

Do you hear the words coming out of my mouth? This question was made popular a few years back, from the movie Rush Hour where Chris Tucker starred with Jackie Chan. In that movie, Chris Tucker's character was explaining to Jackie Chan's character that he was not understanding him because he kept saying something opposite of what Chris wanted to hear, and so he asked him:

"do you hear the words that are coming out of my mouth," There was an understanding issue and a language barrier, so basically they differed on the process which they were approaching communication.

Today, when we talk about do you hear the words that are coming out of my mouth it is literally do you hear the words that are coming out of my mouth, and as you hear those words you want to be clear that hearing those words means that we want to give up of ourselves to another person. We want to clear up the situation when we do not hear what the other person is saying, when we do not hear what the person is actually saying, when we do not check for what's being said and done and when we are not looking for the best out of another person, so basically do you hear the words that are coming out of my mouth.

There are times when I say certain things and I want to take them back, but you cannot take words back once they left the threshold of your mouth. You want to but you're not able to. What we should do and consider is what happens before you say them. This phrase says, 'think before you speak.' Think about the words that are going to come out of your mouth and before you speak them. Our text goes into some very pointed words and that is why we are doing one scripture today, because this one scripture is going to take us a while.

WHOLESOME DEFINED

The first thing we want to do today is define unwholesome according to dictionary.com, unhealthy, deleterious to help a physical or moral being, not sound and health, unhealthy especially in appearance and justice of disease, it is an adjective, which means it is a describer of another word so it says unwholesome talk. The adjective there describes the type of talk that we are into, and you know I'm an author, so some grammatical influence is had here although I refuse to teach English, but that is another term and another subject for another time. Understand that unwholesome is unhealthy, it is degrading, it is a put down, it is typically malicious, not positive, definitely negative. As we apply that definition, when you consider the words that come out of my mouth, how would you grade yourself? There are occasions when we have an opportunity to look at others and judge them for what they're wearing, or what they're doing or what they've done and we really need to be careful about that. There are times I find myself strong enough to steer the conversation in a different direction, and other times I find myself right there in the midst of it, sometimes even starting the dialogue but overall this is designed to uplift.

GUARD THE WORDS WHICH COME OUT OF MY MOUTH

We want to start with the concept of guarding those words that spring from your mouth. How do I guard the words that come out of my mouth? As I mentioned earlier, think before you speak. Next is probably the most important piece of advice, ask yourself how this is going to be received when it comes out of my mouth, and would I say it if other people were standing here, starting with Jesus, maybe your children, your parent, or even your spouse or mate. Would you say these same things if there were other witnesses around? If that answer is no, it is not likely that you should say it. What if I was provoked? You have control over that provocation. You have control over being provoked. It is something that you can handle and take care of or mange. Likewise, you want to be sure that you also know that if you ever heard those words come out of someone else's mouth regarding you, how are you going to feel? We are going to look at the deeper meaning of what kind of response would it stir. How are you really going to feel?

I want to remind us today that our words have power. Proverbs 18:21 says: The tongue has the power of life and death. So that power needs to be properly placed, properly positioned, properly used. This popular phrase is, 'am I my brother's keeper.' The only way you can be that persons keeper is to be able to assist them in their growth and the only way to assist them in their growth is to be able to undergird and uplift them. So I have to be able to know and offer some positive activity toward this person. I have to offer some positive word to this person, if I intend to be able to be a watchful eye.

I was just having a dialogue about an accountability partner and we should all have one. In the conversation of accountability partners, the questions you ask your accountability partners are: have you prayed, studied or meditated today; and 2, accomplished one thing on your goals sheet. This is not a gossip session. Can it be a friend? Absolutely, but should not be required. The accountability partner lends itself to the fact that you have a relationship with this individual, but they do not necessarily have to be a friend.

Words Which Break

Unwholesome talk are words that break; breaks your spirit. Most of us are running around frail anyway, one wrong wind can blow, and we are crying, or dying, down or depressed. One wrong word could be the straw that breaks the camel's back, or something that tips the pendulum in the wrong direction, and everything can go awry. There is an adage which states that hurt people hurt people.' We do not want to perpetuate that, we want to stop that typical effect of people hurting other people and those people hurt the next person. We want to stop that, so let's start with our selves.

I recall a time when I said some things to you that could bring you to tears between my look and my presence, my voice and my tone, including the words that came out of my mouth. I could stir up things inside of another individual; that is nothing to be proud of, and I say that in a repented manner. I give more focus on what my words can do and then God showed me what my words can do. He has allowed me to publish thirty-five books where I uplift, upgrade, enhance, encourage, enrich, energize and inspire others to do the things they desire to do and now know that it is possible because I reiterated what God already told us.

WORDS WHICH BUILD

When you give credence to those types of things, and you yield audience to those types of things, you're going to ask yourself how to get yourself back to a place where you once were concerned about the feelings of another and so much so that you gave them exactly what it is they were in need of and at that particular point of their needs. You stood there in the gap for them. You took care of those needs for them. We want to avoid words that break, avoid words which burden, avoid words that just hurt, and measure those opportunities carefully. We are in each other's paths for a reason and you want to do your job.

Of course, we want to move into words that build, but only when it is helpful for building others up. Only what is helpful for building others up. For example: you look great, that was an awesome word, thank you for your encouragement, thank you for being a blessing to me, thank you for being obedient and being in your place so that I can be blessed. Those are things I tell people who do that for me. Build them up and encourage them, ask them about themselves: what are your goals? Is there any way I can help you reach them? Is it connecting them with someone who can help them with that situation. 'I know that you're down right now, but it is not going to always be that way' versus 'well you should have . . .' We can always tell someone what you should have done. Why is it that we say that? Why? Words that build.

WORDS WHICH BOND

Words which bond: I love you; I think about you; I consider you; you'e on my mind; you're weighing heavily on my heart; is there anything I can do to help you? I really mean those things, and follow up and do those things. When I teach about love, I share with people that love is a verb. I love you is a verb. People often confuse that as an expression, or misuse it, or do not consider it, or never really realize it is a verb. That verb means that there's an action that accompanies that, that verb means there is a message that goes with that word. That message needs a line of hope. I do things to show you that I love you through my actions and behavior and not just the words "I love you." That needs to be a match up and quite honestly I want to be clear about the fact that when you love someone, you love them at their level, for what they ask, for how to be loved, not just the way you want to love them, but the way they need to be loved, or how they want to be loved, that is how they know you love them by what you express to their filter, their definition and their expectations.

WORDS WHICH BIND

Words which bind. Binding when we consider the definition and the contextual way that it is used. Binding that which knits things together, to fasten or secure, to encircle, to bondage, to fasten around, to tie up, things that are bond, things what you bind. Typically, people think of it as a legal term and things that are bind to the others, such as a binding agreement, which means you're legally obligated to complete whatever the task is. So, we want words that bind, that attach you to me, that secure us in a bond, that encircle us, and engage us to one another. I cannot firmly do that if I'm having to share ugly words with you any unwholesome talk with you. I cannot do that.

Don't take comfort in the words 'I told the truth and love,' but whose definition of truth and love was that? She's standing there crying, ready to do things to herself that are illegal, she's resorted to her 'go-to,' and you thought that what you said in love, not so much. Let's define that and stop using that as the excuse that we use when you decide to tell somebody off, or tell somebody like it is. Just tell us that you are going to tell it like it is because I'm hurting, and I'm feeling bad. Let us know that. Just be honest with yourself and let us know that, but only when it helps to build others up according to their needs.

In order to know another person's needs, you're going to learn that from two sources. The first one the Holy Spirit, number two out of their own mouth. In the first instance, you have to be sensitive enough to the Holy Spirit that you have taken this information to the Lord through prayer, maybe even fasting. You want to be able to say to this person that you have loved them, tried to take care of them, been all that you know to do for this person. 'Lord, show me how to give them what they need according to their needs and according to Your will through what I can contribute to their lives' is a tall order that would be the Lord's request. You have to be able to stay in the fight, you cannot give up or quit, it has to be something you give diligent time to. There are some people that are very sensitive to that. A couple of my friends are very sensitive to that, there are very few people who can just determine what emotion Onedia needs. It is not very often that it happens, and definitely not very often in a scenario where one can say, 'I have been able to identify what are your needs and, I'm able to take action on that.'

Likewise I'm the type of person that when I tell you what I need, I really mean that. I personally do not depend on many people, so when I need you to do something, it is not something that I've asked for lightly. It is not something I've asked for without thought and without prayer, and without avoiding asking you.

Do know that I've done all that I can to avoid asking you to do something for me, because I do not want to be disappointed. I do not ask other people to help me because I do not want to be disappointed. I do understand when others do not ask for help either. I often surprise people when I go beyond what I need to or what I can do to assist another individual. Ask yourself when you're looking at someone according to their needs, do you know what those needs are, have you been listening to that person, and do they believe that you can and really will help them. Do what it is you say you're going to do, again words which bind. Words which break we are going to avoid, words which we are going to focus on, words which bind we are going to start to identify you and words which bind, we are going to exercise and engage and complete, and finally words which benefit, that it may benefit those who listen.

WORDS WHICH BENEFIT

I mentioned to you that I've written a number of books, those words will live far beyond my lifetime. Those words were taken from my heart, they are an authentic part of who I am, and they are designed to be beneficial to those around me and it only started because of two little people. Initially because I needed an outlet. I needed to encourage myself. I needed to see some words that were great among those things that I wrote, and among those things I've written. I needed something to overshadow that negativity that I was taking in from the outside world but it all started with me, it was for me. And there was so much that I determined that I need to share it. I was now driven by the fact that I needed to give them away the others. Likewise, I gave it to my children and so clearly understand that we have the give some thought to where we head next; we have to give some thought to what we do next. We have to give some thought to what happens in our lives and we want to say, 'hey when I give out these words that benefit,' actually it benefits you both, whoever heard you, and it benefits you. Those words that we use that benefit are going uplift, upgrade, enhance, lead a relationship, leave a model, do all those things for the purpose of bringing that person out of the storm they're in, it is going to help them understand who they are and who they're expected to be. It is going to put you in a position where you can say, 'you know what I heard myself speak and I can use those words I shared myself, let me go see about my business,' and that happens often to me.

When you put yourself in a position where you say, 'hey I want to be a blessing to someone else,' it is a definite situation where you want to give credence to the things that are about you, important to you, that are informational for you and when you do that, you want to feel better about who you are because you are able to encourage the next person, you are able to deliver to the next person something you had not previously considered and you definitely want to do that. You definitely want to give to the next person exactly what God has given you to give to them.

We also find out that when we give words that benefit , that it did not cost us anything extra to share in a loving manner how to get past this point, I like giving myself to others, I do not lose anything at all. When I teach, when I share, when I help and when I pray for, I do not lose anything. I gain so much more. There are times people say, 'I had to work hard to get that information, they should too.' Not necessarily. You have gone through the bad stuff to help somebody, and you went through the good stuff, to help the same group of people, it takes all of it, it is a full experience, you share which is freely openly and willingly. Therefore, you're taking care of them as you should, then somebody is going to come along and take care of you, but if you're not willing to give and hand is closed nobody can put anything else in it especially not God, God gives to those and blesses those He can bless through, He also designed for you to share, you're not going to run out. I made mention of not running out of love; I said that your love tank cannot be empty because you're not going to run out of love. A friend of mine laughed and I said, 'why are you laughing, it is not funny. You're not going to run out. Give it away, Jesus is standing by with a replenishment system, that you yourself cannot even detect, He's going to give you more to be able to give more to someone else.' The fact of the matter is that you are making others work for love when it was freely given and undeserved when it was given to you. And you are also given love to give away. But you will not.

So words which break. Words which build, bond, bind and words which benefit should be the words coming out of your mouth. We want to consider and make sure that we are blessing those around us, do not let any unwholesome talk come out of your mouth, but only when it is helpful to others according to their needs, that it may benefit those who listen. We often get to a very comfortable place in our lives, when we think this is not about us, but it absolutely is.

The King James version says, 'it minister grace unto the hearer.' Those are two powerful words: minister grace. Your words can help someone stay alive. Use the words that come out of your mouth to give them a new hope because that is what we are designed to do.

Lord God, how we thank You and we love You for this day, this word, this message. Let us abide and those words today and we may be able to share with others how to benefit them and help them use that power to raise the level of their lives and get them closer to You. Lord God, I thank You for what You have done for me. In Jesus name we pray. Amen and thank God.

A Sacrificial Love
Ephesians 5:25-30 (NKJV)

²⁵ Husbands, love your wives, just as Christ also loved the church and gave Himself for her, ²⁶ that He might sanctify and cleanse her with the washing of water by the word, ²⁷ that He might present her to Himself a glorious church, not having spot or wrinkle or any such thing, but that she should be holy and without blemish. ²⁸ So husbands ought to love their own wives as their own bodies; he who loves his wife loves himself. ²⁹ For no one ever hated his own flesh, but nourishes and cherishes it, just as the Lord *does* the church. ³⁰ For we are members of His body, of His flesh and of His bones.

Ephesians 5:25-30 (NKJV)

Lord God, how we thank You and how we love You this day for what we'll learn, and what we'll discover, what You will uncover for us at this time. Lord God, we thank You for this time that's shared with You, and we thank You, Lord, for having a sacrificial love for each and every one of us. And Lord, we thank You right now for Your power, Your strength, Your might, Your courage, and all of what is required to love someone completely and diligently and whole. Lord remind me not to be selfish. So, Lord, as we discover and uncover what is in the scripture text this evening, Lord God, I thank You right now for giving us what You have for us today, so our daily bread, and it is unto you that we submit to all of that. It is in Your Son, Jesus' name that we ask His blessings in this prayer. Amen.

Ephesians was penned by Paul and Paul is all about love. He wants you to understand love, and define love, and be part of what love is, and he wants you to be engrossed in love and to take part in love at a big level so that we can all be clear about what His design for us is. Paul wants us to understand that. So in this sacrifice, he wants us to understand that a significant measure of love is the relationship these scriptures share.

Now, when you talk about a significant measure of love, you want to understand that Christ gave up His life for the church. He gave it up for the church so that we may be made complete and whole. And one question I have is, can we do it? Can we give up a significant measure of love? Can we give another person a significant measure of love as described in these scriptures? And the answer is yes, we can. And as a matter of fact, we're only equipped to love this way, and anything less than all is our way of a self-defense mechanism. We take that self-defense mechanism because of what happened when we were not a recipient of the same sacrificial love these words describe. Maybe we were hurt, maybe we were pushed aside, maybe we weren't embraced the way we thought we should have been.

All in all, we want to ensure that we are in a position to love at the right level. And the only level to love at is at the highest level. A sacrificial love.

These scriptures open up with one of the most— it would come to be one of the most offensive words in the English language: Submit. And I didn't cover those preceding verses, but it bears mentioning because it becomes such a bad word. Because it becomes such a bad word, we have to give it a little bit more encouragement, because in order to actually sacrifice at the level that Christ sacrificed for the church, submission is required. And we have to remind ourselves, we're not submitting to humans. We get caught up thinking that we're submitting to humans when we're actually submitting to God. When we get to a point where we can't remember that we're submitting to God, then we then have an additional problem.

That particular problem is going to give us things that we're not completely able to contend with. He is the One who equips us to submit. He is the One who designs the person who we're supposed to submit to. He is the person who does those things, and He is going to be the person who is able to say to us, 'it is okay to submit right here.' The word has become dirty because people do not understand that that submission is unto the Lord and not unto a human being. And the person who feels that they should be submitted to takes advantage of that situation. And then that becomes the problem.

We want to get away from thinking that people are to submit unto us. That is not why or what— that is not the way that is supposed to happen. The submission is designed by God, and it really comes through us. We have to be careful on thinking the things that were designed as a submissive tool— that we take advantage of those things. We want to make sure that we don't find ourselves in that situation.

A lot of women find themselves having trouble getting married, because they feel like they have to submit, that they have to give up something of themselves. And that is true, but that giving up of something of yourself doesn't take anything from you. It really should enhance you.

I want to talk about that sacrificial love so that we put down our defense mechanism. I wrote a poem about this called Unlock Fort Knox. And I suggest the imagery and the metaphor of Fort Knox because we are so fixed on being able to put ourselves first. We're so set on, 'I'm not going to submit to another individual.' We're so set on being independent that we cannot see the benefit of a sacrificial love.

WITH NOTHING TO LOSE

When you give yourself away, you don't lose anything. Giving yourself away so that He can continue to be fulfilled, and so that you can continue to be filled, is the objective of this love. This is not— it's not a goal without God's guidance.

Let's look at verse 25: "Husbands, love your wives, just as Christ also loved the church and gave Himself for her."

This was demonstrated first by Christ. When Christ gave His life on the cross for us to have life and have it more abundantly, to have it eternally, He gave up things for us. And because He gave up those things for us, we want to be sure that we understand why He did that. He did that to fulfill the promises of God. Because He did that, we have to do our part as well.

And this is given to husbands, but this is a global message. The type of sacrificial love that we're talking about is one that we should share with the people around us. Again, you don't lose anything by loving at this level, you just don't. This is something that we should consider an asset versus a liability. And you don't lose anything by this.

WHAT ARE YOU WILLING TO GIVE

This sacrificial love requires you to give up something. But what are you willing to give up? Well, the first thing most of us understand about love is that this is a verb, and time is required. We want to ensure that we make certain that we don't do things that people are going to find, if you will, offensive. But we also want to be sure that we understand that, I'm here because I like to spend time with you. I'm here because I want your time. I want time that you could've been doing something else with; I want that time. I want to be able to get to you in the type of time that you would normally give to something else. I want that time.

When we ask ourselves, who do we give our time to? To what do we share our time? We have to look into that and say, well, I spend my time on this. But you want the time I spend on that. And that is going to be the point where we have to say to ourselves, what's more important television, reading, shopping, gardening, or my loved ones? We have to decide what's most important.

Hillary Weeks sings a song that says, if I only had today. And she goes on to go through a litany of things she would do differently. She would leave the dishes in the sink. If I only had today. Well the truth is that every day should be treated like we only have today. What we find ourselves doing is putting off for tomorrow what we should be working on today. We have no problem with it because we feel like what we've done is okay, because we're doing this because of that person, we're doing that because of this person. We're doing this because we think this is what they want. However, if you really ask that person, what is important to you? And when they start to tell you, it has nothing to do with all that you have or all that you're looking for. It has nothing to do with those things. Yet it has everything to do with being healthy and whole. It has everything to do with getting what they need to them. Most of it is going to be time.

Dr. Gary Chapman has written several books about the five love languages, and he contends that there are five love languages that everybody should have at least one of. If you love that person in their love language, you'll have a better relationship. The truth of the matter is that you have to ask yourself very carefully, am I doing all that I can to make that a reality? Am I doing what I should be doing to find out what my mate's love language is? And then be able to take that love language and use it effectively in order to love them. That's going to require some sacrifice. Part of that sacrifice is finding out what that is. Well, don't you think they know their love language? Not all the time.

But it is our job as we love someone to occupy that space of their love languages, and love them the way they need to be loved, and love them the way they want. And when you say to me, 'well, I've done everything that I know to do for this person;' 'did you ask them how they wanted to be loved?' The answer is normally no, and my question is, when are you going to ask? Because right now, they want to be loved in their language. And the only way to get to love them in their language is to pay attention to who they are. That's what could be the key to everything that you do is getting them to the point where they appreciate being loved on their level, at their level, for them.

So ask yourself, 'am I able? Am I able to do this? Am I able to love them at such an incredible level that they are able to love and be loved, and understand that they are being loved at the highest possible level?' But we've got to get there. That sacrificial love is going to require you to give up something, and you've got to figure out what that something is going to be.

WHEN YOU GIVE LOVE TO OTHERS, THEY ARE MADE WHOLE

Secondly, when you give love to others, they are made whole. Loving them improves their status, cleanses them, and helps them forge ahead. Showering another with your love does not actually cost you anything. And I want to talk about that for just a moment. It doesn't cost you anything to love another person, because you are not the giver, author, creator, orchestrator, or the provider of anything at all. And certainly you're not the originator of love. You didn't create love, you don't define love. As a matter of fact, you actually altered the definition in a detrimental way, personally. But once we get back to the Originator, the Creator, the Designer, the defining moment of love, we can use that to measure all love that is taking place.

You see, we think that we make a decision about what love is, and that actually is not true. It couldn't be further from the truth. We have to use the definition we were given, which is God and Jesus Christ. Upon using that definition, that lets us understand that it's not costing me anything, because He actually gives love to me to give it to you. He didn't give it to me just for myself; He gave it to you. He gave it to me to give to you. It doesn't cost you anything because you're not filling yourself.

Again, back to Dr. Gary Chapman. He talks about a love tank, and he talks about that fact that your spouse and your loved ones around you, their responsibility is to keep that love tank full. And that's true. It's our responsibility, in order for the love tank to be kept full, to participate at a very high level where we tell you when the love tank is empty, or emptying, or needs to be refilled. Do you understand yourself enough in order to be able to have that kind of conversation. But here's the thing— that was the human side. The catch is going to be with God. With God, He knows that you're love tank is empty. He knows when it needs to be filled, and He has an automatic replenish.

I used to be the store manager of a GAP, and we had a system that knew at headquarters when something in my store had been sold. Because the system knows when it had been sold, it was replaced by the automatic replenishment system until the distribution center runs out. Well the problem is, is that our Distribution Center is Jesus Christ, and His replenishment bucket is never going to run empty. He's never going to run out. And that's the good news, that's the great news, and that's when we need to celebrate. That's when we need to drop anchor. That's when we need to pause and have a spiritual moment right there, because what I just said was His love is not like the clothing at the distribution center, nor does He give love when He feels like it or because He thought it over, or because He thought about it, or because I deserved it. He did not give me love because He thought it was a good time to give me love. He gave me love because He knew I needed it right then. He didn't forget. He didn't leave it at the store. He didn't forget it on the porch. He gave me love right then, deposited it right into my love tank, and He keeps it full, and I am typically drinking from a saucer underneath because my cup is overflowing.

He doesn't give out our love in a conditional fashion. He gives it to us on an as-needed, before-needed, abundantly-when-necessary love. And while we're being honest with ourselves, we aren't giving out enough love for Him to even ever need to do a whole bunch of replenishing anyway, because some of us are so selfish about love, we think that we are doing someone a favor when we are doing ourselves a disservice. We've got to keep that in mind. Love is the thing He gives to us to give to other people; He didn't give it to you to keep. It's not for you to harbor. It's not for you to hold on tight to. It is for you to give away. It is not designed for you to keep held up and captive, and held in some type of a jar to be used in case of emergency. Every day houses an emergency which requires love. It is to be used daily with everyone who crosses your path.

We have a rule, in retail: if you are within two to three feet of me, I have to approach you. Those are the same rules that should be with love. If you get into my presence, if you're related to me, if you're someone I know, if you're someone who I'm going to come in contact with who I don't know, then guess what? You are to be loved by me in some form or fashion. You are to be loved by me.

So when we consider the fact that we think that when we give our love away, it is going to cost us or that we're going to be doing someone a favor or we're going to take something from ourselves, we need to remind ourselves, we did not create this; He did. And we're not the orchestrator of these relationships; He is. He decides who crosses our path and when, why are we there and for what reason and for what length of time. He orchestrates why we're the person that we are to be in each other's presence, and we need to recognize that for exactly what it is. We've got to recognize that we need to do for others that which we do for ourselves.

Verses 28 through 30 read: "So husbands ought to love their own wives as their own bodies; he who loves his wife loves himself. For no one ever hated his own flesh, but nourishes and cherishes it, just as the Lord does the church. For we are members of His body."

The golden rule springs to mind; do unto others as you would have them do unto you. But I think that we need to take the golden rule and add something to it. Do unto others as you would have them, or want them, above all else, to do for you. Treat them like Christ treats you. Do more for them than they will ever do for you. Do for them what you do for yourself, and if that's horrible then we need to seek an upgrade on both parts.

WITH SACRIFICE, I LOVE

You see, there's that part where He says that the second command is love your neighbor as yourself. The reason we have a problem loving others and loving others sacrificially is we don't give a flip about our own selves. We don't care about who we are. We don't love ourselves. We can't get past some things; we can't forgive ourselves. In order to love, there has to be forgiveness. If you can't love yourself, and that's why you can't love someone else, then you need to forgive, love ourselves, sweep on our own front porches, and learn to love and give up and give those things away. Give them back to God, our burdens, to give them back to God so we can love others as we should love ourselves. But until that time, from this time to that, just make it your business not to hate, not to share disdain, not to quarrel, not to complain. Share that time, and that is on the pathway back to love. Some of us need to get past some things before we can really love, and that's fine. But you need to put a short leash on that; we're talking about two or three days at the most. You need to be loving somebody by Friday. And I really mean that. Of this week. That is my message of urgency.

So understand that we've got to get past the point of conditional love in order to get to some places differently than where we've ever been. And because we have never been some of these places before, we've got to act like and understand that we are in a different situation where things are now different. And we want to say that they're different, but we really want to act differently. So we need to get ourselves to a place where we can love sacrificially, and to be able to give ourselves to God like we should. Because He's looking for us and expecting for us to perform at that level, because we are the Christians, and it's Him who is taking the risk.

As I stated earlier, I want us to be sure that we understand, number one, we give our love away. We don't lose anything. It doesn't cost us anything. We're never going to run out of the love that God gives to us to give to others. We're never going to run out. We need to stop acting so stingy and selfish, and give it away as we should. When we give our love to others, we help them become whole. We remind them that there is a Christ. We improve their disposition and we give them hope. We give them a reason to divorce their disdain and to come forward to allow Christ to love them. And when we do for others that which we do for ourselves, and upgrade them one in the same, we've got to ask ourselves, is this what Christ would want me to love myself like? Would He approve of me treating myself with this type of mediocrity, and treating others the same way? The answer is absolutely not.

Learn to operate under the sufficiency of His total grace. The total sufficiency of His grace is one of those things where you've got to give yourself an opportunity to love and to be loved by gracious God Our Father. And allow us to do the same. There's a freedom to love.

I would ask you to spend some time on First Corinthians 13, and I did this exercise many years ago, but then it still has the same power as it did then. It is an exercise that involves you putting your name in the spots that says "love." And so it would say something like this: Onedia is patient and Onedia is kind. Onedia does not boast and Onedia does not envy."

And as you go on and on, you understand how you are supposed to behave, and you are supposed to be the noun in that sentence. And you're supposed to be love and the definition thereof. You have to behave a certain way, and you can't let anybody get you out of the habit of the desire to love, the efficiency, and the effectiveness of love. Because love is effective. It has an efficiency. It has a level of grace that goes with it, and it is a huge influence over another person's life. I ask for you to try it. I hope that you really will.

Lord God, we thank You for this day, for this hour. We thank You for Your definition of love, Your demonstration of love. We hope that we are better of it, and we're better for it, and we're nonetheless never going to be empty of Your love, never going to be bored of Your love. You demonstrated that back on cavalry a couple of thousand years ago, and so Lord God, we thank You right now for being able to renew that spirit of love within us, and love without concern of what's going to happen on the other side, if that person may not love us back. Lord God, we thank You right now that You understand who we are. Lord God, knowing that giving our love away is just par for the course. It's what You call us to do, and You've given us the tools to get it done. And oh Lord God, I thank You, I thank You for forgiving us of our sins. I thank You for loving us unconditionally. In Your Son Jesus' name, we pray. Amen.

A Sign, A Signal, and A Solution
Exodus 40:33-38

³³ Then Moses set up the courtyard around the tabernacle and altar and put up the curtain at the entrance to the courtyard. And so Moses finished the work.

The Glory of the LORD

³⁴ Then the cloud covered the tent of meeting, and the glory of the LORD filled the tabernacle. ³⁵ Moses could not enter the tent of meeting because the cloud had settled on it, and the glory of the LORD filled the tabernacle.

³⁶ In all the travels of the Israelites, whenever the cloud lifted from above the tabernacle, they would set out; ³⁷ but if the cloud did not lift, they did not set out—until the day it lifted. ³⁸ So the cloud of the LORD was over the tabernacle by day, and fire was in the cloud by night, in the sight of all the Israelites during all their travels.

Exodus 40:33-38 (NIV)

A sign, a signal, and a solution. Moses and God had been in an intimate relationship from inception and this just continues their relationship and makes Moses do things that seem unorthodox. Things that seem to be unexplainable, that seem to be not the norm and giving people something to be confused about from time to time, or maybe all the time.

Remember he just got the second set of tablets completed, after he dropped the first ones. And now God is explaining to him when we move and how we move.

The Sign

The sign, the cloud, and for our understanding we have to realize that this cloud is overhead, and when the cloud moves from over the tabernacle they can move. While the cloud is there they have to remain in place. Now, this is a sign for what they can and cannot do.

Verse 34-35 reads: 'while the cloud covered the tent of meeting and the glory of the Lord filled the tabernacle, Moses could not enter the tent of meeting because the cloud had settled on it and the glory of the Lord filled the tabernacle.'

So while the glory of the Lord is in the tabernacle, hence that Glory and Moses cannot occupy the same space. This sign is only relative to them being able to understand when or how they could move.

Now, the sign of the clouds. I live in Houston, Texas, so on any given day, we can have all weather behaviors in the same afternoon. And it sounds crazy but it could be cool in the morning. Cool really col, like 45 degrees. And by noon it could be 95. And then it could drop significantly to the 30s at night. Sometimes our weather is that radical. It's that tumultuous. Well inside of that whole concept, all we can say is the weather is at God's hands. Likewise, this cloud is at His hands. This sign of the cloud gives the Israelites clear direction.

Now, I do not know about you, but that is all I want to do is get clear cut direction from God. When do I move? When do I go? When do I stay? How long do I say? How far do I go? The cloud solved all of that for them. The cloud gives them significant information about how to make those decisions. The cloud was over the tent where they reside. If the cloud moves and is lifted, they can go.

Now understand, this group of individuals have been traveling for a long time. It is my hope that because they have been traveling together a long time, they know each other's movements. I hope that they know each other's thought processes. I hope that they know each other's navigational efforts. I hope that they know these types of things. Because I think they should know, I hope that they are using their knowledge of one another to make the best move they possibly can make. However, I know just like in families, we do not move when another person says to move because they aren't the boss of me. Well see, the cloud solved that. The cloud delivered by the Boss of us tells us when to move because that is when the Boss of us wants us to move.

So the cloud can be lifted for 10 minutes, 10 days, 10 hours. And at that point you have to move. Now realize that you are mobile because you are traveling to a land God has prepared for you. You are not in your permanent place. This is not just moving around town. This is moving long distances. For them, they take everything with them every time they move.

My question as I was doing my studies is what signs has God given you about when to move and when to stay? You see we are technically disobedient. Born into sin and iniquity, so our obedience level is a little subjective. Our signs are not as clear as the cloud overhead. We can say we think it is and for the purpose of your situation it may be. But everybody did not get a cloud. Some people got a nudge. Some people got an invitation to walk on water. Some people got to touch His cloak. They are invitations to move. He asked a man by the pool, Jesus did. "Do you want to walk?" That was his sign. Without further ado he gets up and grabs his mat and keeps it moving.

What is the sign that you have been given? What does your sign look like? And what we want to be careful of is that we do not make up our own signs. We do not make up our own assumptions. We do not move on our own situations. We do not make up our own scenarios. What we want to be able to do, is look for the sign that is most indicative of God. Is it going to seem utterly ridiculous? It might. Is it going to be out of the box, out of the norm for what you would do? Quite possibly. But all in all it is a sign. It is a sign to indicate that God is overhead. God is in control. God is managing the circumstance and the situation. God is doing all that God needs to do to be God and to provide for you. He did not forget about you when you had to stay there 10 minutes longer than what you thought. Yes, I did say 10 minutes. Yes, there are times in our situation that we want to be in a hurry. We want the situation to end just about immediately. Then when it's not immediate, we do not understand why. We do not understand why not. We are clearly consumed and concerned with the wrong things. What does that look like? How do we get past that point in our situation? How do we get past the wrong things? How do we get past worrying about the wrong things? Using the wrong sign to make a decision?

There are times in our lives when we look at something and say well that has to be God. But it's really a distraction. That has to be God but that is a similar but different distraction. 'Onedia, why is it similar but different?' Its similar in that it distracted you. And so different that it shouldn't have. It swung so far to the left of that original distraction that it should have also been labeled that distraction. God is not that kind of God. What we see as extraordinary to us is ordinary to Him. But some of those things that we think should be Him are profanely against His whole will. And we do not consider that. Your sign is going to be ordered.

When God indicated that He sent the cloud Initially, I'm sure there was some confusion. Do we follow this for real? Do we really do this? But at the end of the day, once he got everybody acclimated to this is the word of God. This is a sign from God. This is what God sent us. Then we realize that then we have to follow it. And that is where we get mostly into trouble. We look at the sign and then we say, 'well that wasn't for me.' When in fact it really is for you, and we are waiting on you to get in your position under the cloud and move in sync with the cloud.

THE SIGNAL

Moses had it hard a little bit. I feel a little bit sorry for Moses. The Glory of the Lord filled the tabernacle. And when the glory of the Lord is inside the tabernacle, and still in the tabernacle, Moses cannot enter it. But did not you just want to be Moses just to see what the tabernacle looked like when it was filled with God? When it was completely filled? No ugly inside. No problems inside. No issues inside. None of that. And so because of His filling of the tabernacle, because His indwelling of the tabernacle, Moses could not go in. But did not you want to be able to stand there, and just look at the place where God filled? How would it feel to be standing in a place completely filled by God? How would it feel to be in a place that has such intimacy with God? How would it feel where you to be just be in a place where you could sit and feel the glory of God and not be mistaken about the glory of God? You knew that place held the glory of God. In as much as God allowed It to be held in this edifice. Just the thought of those questions overwhelms me. Just the thought of that concept overrides my spirit and allow me to understand that it was because God allowed it. Now Moses couldn't enter because it would have been too powerful for Moses.

He indicates in Exodus in an earlier chapter, 'I am going to pass by you. And you can just look at Me from the back. Because you can't handle seeing the total of Me. You just can't do it.' When you talk about the glory of God, can we handle it all? There is a song called I need Your glory. The lyrics are: 'I want Your glory. Less of me and more of You is what I need. Show me Your glory. Show me Your power.' And what I need is sometimes not what I want. Is it really what I want? Do I want to deny myself daily care and my cause to follow Jesus? Am I willing to pay the cost it contains to be in His likeness completely? Am I willing and ready to do it for real? The whole point of it all is, can we do exactly what we have been called to do, in the time that we have been called to do it, based on the sign and the signal that we received?

We want to be able to do those things. And we can only do those things if we are paying attention to the signs. And we are sensitive to the signals. Now, of course that is going to bring me to some intimate questions for us today. What is the signal that God is giving? And then my question what is He giving you? And how do you know it's from Him? How do you know it's of Him? What indications do you have that Lord this is you?

I recently facilitated a class called Discerning the Voice of God. We have to learn how to hear His voice. Hearing His voice and being able to follow His direction comes hand in hand. There are going to be times when we think we hear His voice, but that was really us. A Christian comedian said that sometimes we have indigestion and you hope it was God but really it was not. Understand that we have to be able to hear Him. Hear Him clearly. Visualize Him clearly. Get intimate with Him on a very intimate basis. Because at the end of the day, every day, when you get on your knees and pray to the Father. And kneel before the father whom all decedents derive their name, you want to be sure and absolutely clear that you heard from God today. Not some figment of your imagination. Not some false substitute. Not something that you hoped He crossed up with something you wanted. That was really nothing He said at all. God has a way of putting you exactly where He wants you to be, to do the work He wants you to do.

I mentioned this before, but it's worth mentioning again. He knows which of us is going to need the most help with understanding and how to get our attention.

He knows who we are and that we cannot be told what to do. He knows who are who is going to reject the messenger. Our deep intellectual selves would have rejected Moses. We are so 'deep,' we would have told Moses, 'please sit down. Have a seat. Do not talk. We're not going anywhere with you. Because you did this right here and this over there.' Wwe would have been able to document in a corporate fashion what Moses did wrong, which is indicative of us not following Jesus. And so from that day to this, when God has said to us, 'do what it is I need you to do, take care of the things I need you to take care of, and be able to move when I say move,' we always have an excuse and an explanation.

Understand that these people did not live in 4-bedroom, 3,000 square foot homes. For all intents and purposes, they were rather nomadic. They were living in portable tents. They did not have a 30-year mortgage. They eventually got to something that would be similar and have a permanent location, but for the purpose of this scripture text, they were moving when God said to move.

There were not 'things' that inhibited them from making those moves. They did not have to give 2 weeks notices to their job. 'What are you saying to me Onedia, am I not supposed to work? Am I not supposed to provide a home for my family?' No. I am not saying that at all. What I am saying is your life so structured and so put together and so planned and so orchestrated that you put God out of it. Not that you just left God out of your plans, that you put God all the way out. You only want to do things when it is convenient for us. We want to do things when it is convenient to do. And right here right now it is not convenient anymore to serve God. It's not convenient anymore. Why? We get to a point where we think it should be done out of convenience. I want you to know that that signal because that signal could easily be Him shutting all those things down. He can close every one of those doors that you have open. He can close them and He could turn you around so the only person you can talk to deal with, address and request information from is him. In my educated conclusion with my sanctified imagination, with my intelligence, I do not ever want God to do that to me because all the influence you think you have, and all the power you thought you had, and all the influence you think that you can exercise, is gone. Because God wants you where He wants you, in the timeframe He wants you in. All of those other things will just distract you from the original goal, the original plan. That signal is important. So whatever signal He has given to indicate to you what He is trying to get accomplished, you might want to start paying attention to it.

I asked in another sermon what does it take for God to get your attention? What does it take for God to get your undivided, collective attention? What does it take for those things to take place? My answer is going to be something related to I just need to hear from you Lord. We want to say that. We want to say we want to hear from You, Lord. Technically, that is not true. We want to say we want to hear from God. But is that because we want to hear from Him something we want to hear or do we want to hear what He has to say? There is a difference. Because if He says sell all of your worldly possessions and follow Me, some of us are going to say no. Flat out, hands down non-negotiable, and say Jesus please do not say that to me again. You couldn't have been meaning me. You got the wrong address and person.' So we have to be sensitive to the signals.

THE SOLUTION

My third and final point is the solution. The solution is just complete direction. The solution is to the question, 'what are my steps according to Your word? There is no better way to order all of those steps than to use a cloud during the daytime and then there was fire in the cloud by night. So that nobody could say well did the cloud leave? Is it still there? It's still there. It's still right where God intends for it to be. It's right where He called us to be. It's right where He needs us to be right now. It's right where our testimony is going to shine. It's right where our testimony is going to be most effective. It's right where our testimony is going to be most intentional. It's right where He wants us to be at this particular time. In this particular place, doing exactly what He wants us to do. Make no mistake about it. He has given you many gifts. And sometimes He wants you to use them all at the same time. But sometimes He wants you to use one at a time and He indicates which one He wants you to use at a time by where He places you. And when He places you, He is clear about that direction.

I told this testimony several times but it bears repeating. I left a job because I wanted to go somewhere else. I felt my talent would have been better used, better suited somewhere else. So I got another job, I went on and took that job and I was excited. I said, 'this is what I am talking about right here. This is what's hot. This is what I am going to do.' Lo and behold, I ended up, after a series of events, back with the same job and company less than 90 days later. With a promotion, with a raise, and close to my home. In addition to that, God showed me why I wasn't at the other job 9 months later. But He wanted me there. And because He wanted me there, He made provisions for me there. He provided me with those things I indicated plus, He provided me with internal satisfaction of what it is I did. He was able to get me to a point where I could get settled so I could hear from Him because what He did after that was He gave me something else to do. And He had to have me somewhere where I could hear from Him. Know it was Him. I could recognize the sign, the signal and the solution. So He had to put me in that place. For the record, He put me in a place that one year before, I stated emphatically that I would never work, somewhere I had no interest in leading.

Often, people do not understand why we are called to do the things we are called to do. Why we are put in places that we are supposed to be put? Most of the time it is because we would not have gone willingly. But I guarantee you if you ask God why am I here in this location? Why do You have me here in this place? I promise you He will show you. And maybe He uses a cloud, maybe He uses a tent, or maybe He uses a piece of paper. But whatever He uses to show you this is why I have you here, take heed and work while you are there. Because clearly He has you there. And He has work for you to accomplish while you are there.

When I first started teaching, God put me in a school. He put me in that school. That school right there. That was the only job offer I received. He knew He couldn't give me a bunch of choices because I might make my decision on where I needed to be based on the wrong factors. You see, it looked good over there. That was a new school. It had better technology. It had better test scores. And I need to go where better is to be best. Best could be greater. And I like to go where the number one is. I am going double-dutch to number one because I am number one. But He had to show me, 'I need you right here though. Because these kids need some special encouragement that I know you house. I need to open your eyes to some things you are not aware of yet. You are smart and intelligent because I gave you that. That was not of your own doing. No Ma'am. Absolutely not. However, in your all-of-that-ness, you need to see some other things.' Sometimes He does that to us. Sometimes He has to show us that, 'you know, your life was, could have been, it almost looked like this right here. With the wrong right or the wrong left turn. You could have been this kid right here.' And it showed me some things. It helped me understand other people's situation. It helped me understand the nature of education for a child who was 17 in the 8th grade. When I was graduating at 17. Turned 18 in college. I needed to see that. 'I needed you to be drawn into where your deepest passion and your deepest calling had nothing to do with children that are already gifted and talented. It doesn't take a rocket scientist to teach them. But I need somebody that is going to dig into their hearts jump on the boundaries of their hearts and love them because they are My children and you are going to educate them as a bonus.' I said, 'me Lord? You picked me?' 'I picked you. I picked you to do that. I picked you to do that because I know I can trust you. That you are going to do exactly what it is I am telling you to do. Go love those kids and educate them. With the zeal and the zest that you give Me when you teach My word at church.' I said, 'for real Lord?' And He said, 'absolutely.' I said, 'alright if that is what You want. I am in twice.' And from that day to this I have done everything I can to teach kids who are not believers in themselves, thus that disbelief in themselves has blocked their education.

So we have to look for the signs. Make sure they are signs from God. It is His sign indicating that He is there. He has taken residence. He is housed right there. Look for the signal. Where is His glory being housed? How are you going to be the houser? And the housing for His glory as well? You see, those spirits have to recognize each other so it means His dwelling has to be within you as well. And then there is a solution, there is also a direction where He wants us to take course. There is also an ultimate direction where He wants us to do when take that course. So by all means, we want to make sure we are on it.

Lord God, how we bless You. Thank You for this beautiful and wonderful and glorious day. We thank you for doing what you can only do. Lord, I thank You right now for the measure of Your glory. I thank You for the context and the constitution of Your glory. I thank You right now Lord God for who You allow us to be using the tools You have given us. And we thank You for forgiving us when we do not use the tools as exactly You have designed, we use the hammer to crack an egg which is way too much power to get that done. We thank You for allowing us just to be Your children. And we Lord thank You for allowing us to share Your world with others. We thank You right now for the steps that You have chosen right now at this stage and at this hour. And may we go forth exactly how You designed. In Your Son Jesus' name that we ask these blessings and pray this prayer. Amen.

Across Enemy Lines
Ephesians 6:10-12

The Armor of God

[10] Finally, be strong in the Lord and in His mighty power. [11] Put on the full armor of God, so that you can take your stand against the devil's schemes. [12] For our struggle is not against flesh and blood, but against the rulers, against the authorities, against the powers of this dark world and against the spiritual forces of evil in the heavenly realms.

Lord God we thank You right now and how we love You for this day that You have given us and we thank You Lord God for choosing us. When You picked us and chose us, hand crafted us created us, knew us, before You knit us in our mother's womb. Lord God, we thank You for that. Lord God, we thank You for the missions that You have chosen us to carry out and we thank You for what it is You have called us to do in the lives of each other. Lord, we thank You for being obedient and being urged to be obedient in each other's lives. Thank You right now for what it is You called each of us to do and thank You for my answer to that call. Thank You for being receptive to those requests as well. And so Lord God, we thank You right now for what it is You'll have us understand in Your word today. Thank You for the vessel You have chosen to deliver it. Thank You for what You have given to me. Lord God, I thank You, in Your Son Jesus' name we pray and ask His blessings. Amen.

What we consider a fight, we consider the things that we have seen recently regarding war, we have learned that the war was about money, and we have seen it be about stuff. It could be about civil rights, it could be about other people. But when we talk about this particular war, this particular fight, we are talking about ourselves and although you want to understand that this fight is about ourselves, you're fighting against something that you cannot see, that you cannot touch and you might feel the presence of it but you technically cannot feel it. You want to understand this particular fight is not one that you can fight in the physical. It is not a physical fight that someone walks up to you and pushes you on the shoulder and says I want to fight you.

As children, many of us had fights in school because we were challenged about our smarts, about our skin color, our hair or glasses; we were challenged in some fashion. Because in that manner that we were challenged, someone said something to us and they said enough to us to instigate a response. Then you found yourself in a physical fight with another human being. This is so not like that. This is the exact opposite of that. The meaning of this particular fight is going to take place in some different places, this is not a backyard park style fight. This is a fight in your home, in the board room, in the break room, in the retail store, and at church; these are the places with these types of fights will take place.

So one of the things you need to understand about this combat is that there is a such thing as an enemy line. It is the point where you change territories by crossing one particular threshold, one particular place and it may seem like it is not a specific, but technically it is. When you look at the border between here and Louisiana, between here and Oklahoma, you look at those borders and there's a sign that says you are now entering the state of Louisiana, the state of Oklahoma and at the point where you pass that sign, you're now entering into their territory. So when I cross into Louisiana territory, I'm now subject to the laws of that state, the rules of that area. And for all intents and purposes, I need to do what it is that they say. So the speed limit might change, the liquor laws might change, and all the political policies may be different.

I am subject to what they're asking of me and so at the point in which I get there and I am subject to those things, consider that enemy has the same rights. When I cross that bar and I get into enemy territory, that enemy territory becomes my new, becomes my new set of rules, my new family, my new organization. However, nothing like that happens when we are greeted by new people. You see there's no distinct line that says when someone walks up to you and says I'm an enemy. No one does that. We are supposed to be on guard at all times when we come in contact with new people. And they do not always look defensive. But for all intents and purposes, we find that they truly are our enemy.

Recently, I was with some young people, and they taught me this new word called frenemy and I thought it was interesting I asked what that meant they said well it is an enemy posing as a friend. You're close enough to be my friend, but your objective is to harm and the fact that you know this about this individual is the interesting piece and you allow them to hang around. That is a frenemy. Someone who you think is your friend but they turn out to be someone who's not exactly on your side.

Now, our scripture text reads 'Finally, be strong in the Lord and in His mighty power.' We need understand whose mighty power we are under. This mighty power is given to us by God. It is not our own. It is not something that we created ourselves. So we need to understand that we are to use it at His discretion. It was given at is His discretion. Made available at His discretion. In regards to across enemy lines, we need to realize we are in enemy territory and that is not necessarily any fault of our own. 'Well, what do you mean by that, Onedia?' Well, we are in enemy territory and we may not actually with any intention of being there. We may be in enemy territory because the enemy has come to us and surrounded us and encamped around us without our knowledge. 'I find that hard to believe.' It is possible. Because again, the people around you come into contact with you with an opportunity to agree with you, but in the end decide to oppose you. Is that something that you want to be responsible for? The answer then is no.

There's nothing wrong with the fact that the enemy has gotten that close to you because your protection is not of your own, as I mentioned. The text reads be strong in the Lord and in His mighty power. Be strong in the Lord. Not be strong in yourself, not in and of yourself, none of that, it reads be strong in the Lord. You are weak without God.

We want to measure our strength very careful. We never want to overrate our strength or power. And we never want to underestimate the strength and power of our enemy. They come with a certain amount of strength as well. Now, let's understand that the fact that the enemy is designed to attack you. When we consider the book of Job, satan was allowed to attack Job but only to a certain extent. The hand of the Lord is still upon you, He has never left you nor forsaken you. He still provides for you strength and power, even if you're under attack, especially because you're under attack of the enemy. He's aware that you're under attack by the enemy because the enemy had to request permission to attack. Please remember those things when you are whining about, 'well I'm under attack' and 'woe is me.' All of that is true. However, we want to be clear that because we under attack of the enemy, it was designed for us to do some things.

The first thing we do is to recognize that we are in enemy territory and accept the fact that we are there. We can accept that we are there, and because we can accept that we are there, then we can respond appropriately.

Now, the enemy looks familiar. I think that is the most daunting part of this whole thing. We expect our enemies to be people we do not know, people we do not like, and people we do not love. Sometimes it is the exact opposite: it is people we love, it is people we like, and it is people we know. So I want you to understand the concept that the people selected to be used by satan are the regular, normal people that are walking around you. The enemy uses the spirit within people as a mechanism. The devil uses people, satan is going to use somebody, the use of that somebody is going to have access to you in a fashion that you understand that suggests, 'I am being tested by the enemy.'

Verse twelve reads: "for our struggle is not against flesh and blood." We need to understand what that means because of what we want to do in response. You see you're not capable of being the enemy on your own, you have to be asked to be used in that capacity. It tests both persons: the person who's being used by the enemy and then the person who is being tested through the enemy. So then there's always two tests going on. Part of that test will be 'will you recognize that that is the enemy or not;' 'Do you recognize the enemy?' 'Do you realize when you crossed into enemy territory or when the enemy crosses you're your territory?' Did you recognize it?

I often ask people did you consent to let the devil use you. When you consented, how did that make you feel? I am a firm believer that I can ask to not be used by the devil, 'please Lord do not let me be used in that fashion. Please do not let me be used by the enemy to frustrate another individual. Sometimes, we will be used and not even aware. They do things out of character, they do things that lead you to question who they are, and who they really are, did you really know them or not. But what they end up doing is they are tested to see how far they'll go. And to see if they can be continually kept and used by them. Now, that is a dangerous place. That is a dangerous place to be in. But against the ruler, against the authorities against the powers of this dark world and against the spiritual forces of evil in the heavenly realms. The spiritual forces of evil. Again, we are tested such that we might endure.

Now, what we want to be clear about as we are crossing enemy lines is that we are going to need to manage our behavior. Again, the scriptures text teaches us verse 11: put on the full armor of God so that you can take that stand against the devil's schemes. God has provided armor for the protection from these enemies.

There is a law in Texas which said that you are required to wear a seatbelt at all times. Everybody in the vehicle has to have a seat belt on, front seat and back seat, under the age of whatever no longer mattered. Everybody riding in a motor vehicle that was mobile had to wear a seatbelt. That seat belt is designed to protect you if should there be a crash in your vehicle so that no one is as hurt as could have been hurt or killed if you are ejected from the car because you were not wearing a protective device.

As we wander around from day to day, moment to moment, hour to hour, minute to minute, understand that we are wandering in and out of enemy territory, the whole time and the enemy is wandering in and out of our territory, the entire time. God's protection is paramount for that situation. His armor is very necessary and unique for how we handle those incidents. Now, it goes on in verses 12 through 20 to describe what that armor is, what it does, how it was designed, what it is used for, who's to put it on, when, where, how, and why; all of those things are answered in next several verses, the next 8 verses to be exact.

However, for the conversation of our study today, we are not trying to find out what the armor is and what it does, we need to know it exists and the fact that the armor is required. Sometimes we think that we are enemy-free and we can walk around without our armor on. But if you know anything about battle and combat, you know that putting on your armor when the enemy is in your face is too late. The enemy isn't going to stand there and say 'oh I'll wait until you put your protective gear on.' No, they're going to attack you when you're most vulnerable, when you have the armor off, when it is down, when there's one piece open, or when there's one piece that needs to be repaired. You're to put on the full armor every day. So that you can be confident as you take your stance against the devil's schemes. Now that verse assumes that you recognize that the devil was in a scheme and that scheme was aimed at you.

We have to ask ourselves regularly and often and critically about the fact that do we know that we are in a position as Christians, we are the only target of the enemy's schemes. The devil is looking for Christians, he's not looking for anyone else. If you are a non-Christian, you're not going to be attacked by the devil, he's good with you because you're not serving the Lord. But just as sure as your name is what it is and you're determined that you're going to follow Christ no matter what, how, when, where, or why, you are on the top of the list of the devil's schemes, of the devil's target of the frenemy. You're at the very top of that list—it is going to happen. You're going to be at some point under attack. It's not optional. Our behavior is going to dictate how successful this process is. Lest we forget that when we consider why we are tested in this fashion.

Number one, it is a test of whether you will depend on God. It is not by your power your might, it is by the spirit of the Lord that you're able to take a stand against the devil's schemes. It doesn't have to do with your personal self. You're being used for a war aged with God, it is not about you. Wrap your mind around the fact that this is not personal about you. Other people are being attacked as well. So, keep watch over that concept. We want to be a student on watch.

Again, back to the battlefield where the soldiers are sleeping, there are soldiers who are watching. They're encamped around the camp in order to watch for the enemy's approach, so they can be ready to respond to the attack. We have to do that as well, we have to be ready at all times to attack—attack appropriately. And we cannot attack appropriately without wearing the armor. Those six pieces need to be handled very carefully on a regular basis. More importantly, the Author of those six pieces knowing that the Author, the Originator, the Creator of those six pieces are going to require some things from us.

'What are we fighting about, Onedia?' We are fighting for Your soul. We are fighting for your heart. We are fighting for your spirit. We are fighting for your mind. The enemy would love nothing more than to pull you out of the custody of God. And whether you go or not is entirely up to you. The Lord is the strength and the power against this abusive enemy. The Lord is the source of power against this elusive enemy. We have got to remind ourselves as I said before you were not the author or source of your own power. You cannot create your own power, you cannot manage your own power, you cannot add to your own power, or strength; you cannot do those things, you are not the author or orchestrator of those things. You're just not. So, you want to understand the Lord is the Source of strength and of that power. He wants you to ask; He wants to give it to you when you ask of it and as you need it. And sometimes we need it when we do not ask. At times when you're in a position where you wonder what's going on or how is it going or how you're going to make it and He gives you just what you need. Sometimes it's strength, and sometimes it is power, sometimes the combination of the two, however it is going to be what God determines and defines as your personal need at that particular time. You're going to need to understand how to access that power and strength, how to use it wisely, according to His will and His purposes and not get to a point of haughtiness about it.

You cannot claim this strength and power as your own. That is going to be a downfall in the fight. That is going to be the presumptive factor that is going to lead us down the road of what could be a significant path of destruction while we are in the fight. One of the things you want to be able to be sure that we do is not to be elusive during this fight. We want to make sure that we are not passive across enemy lines. We want to make sure we are not producing problems for ourselves across enemy lines. We want to make sure that we are not adding to the issues that we have across enemy lines. We want to make sure that as we are across enemy lines we are doing our very best to handle that process carefully.

We want to fight. We want to use the tools we have in order to fight across enemy lines. As you get across enemy lines you have to ask yourself is this the best possible place for me to be doing what it is I'm doing at this particular time. And so the Lord is going to orchestrate that fight and the agenda for that fight. There are times when we get into a fight and we want to quit. There are times when we get into a fight when we want to walk away. When we want to fight dirty. Won't fight fair. Say the wrong thing. At the wrong time. Do things that are inappropriate. What we need to do is insure that we are in a position where we can say to ourselves we did exactly what we were supposed to do. We want to get ourselves together so that when we get into a situation we can say that we did exactly what the Lord designed me to do as I fought this fight and fighting this fight is going to give you the opportunity to say I am wanting to fight and I want to fight properly. And as I fight properly, then I want to be able to fight where the Lord is impressed with my fight.

Well how do I impress the Lord with a fight that He allowed you the strength and power that He provides because He gave consent for you to be in this situation with people that I thought that I knew, loved, and were close to? Because you go to Him. He will be warm-hearted because you go to Him. And you go to Him in a fashion where you are saying, 'Lord I recognize that I am in a fight and I want Your help with this particular fight. As I gather Your help with this particular fight, Lord God, I want to be able to do for You, with You, through You, and because of You what it is I have been called to fight about.'

With all of that, you want to get yourself in a situation where you say I am in this fight. I want to fight in a fair manner and I want to have the proper equipment, the proper tools and I want to focus on You while I fight. You still need to be able to hear from Him. You still need to be able to access Him. Unlike when we fight across enemy lines, you cannot have any radioactivity because they'll be able to identify your location. We are not in that kind of fight. He is the critical piece to the fight. Focus on Him, never losing sight of Him is a very key factor in the fight. For as we are across enemy lines and we go there, ebb and flow through that process, Lord God, I want to make sure that we are doing the right thing. We want to make sure that we are doing things that we are called upon to do. We want to make sure that we are taking care of the details of the fight. We want to make sure we are not get besides ourselves in the fight and we definitely do not want to claim the victory of a fight that was never ours to begin with.

Across Enemy Lives.

Amen.

Lord God, how we bless You and love You this day. Lord, we thank You for us being on guard for when the fight is on its way. When the fight is over and when the fight is in the midst, when we are in the midst and we promise to give You all the honor praise and glory. We thank You for the fights that we are in. We thank You for the enemies that come in our path. We promise You that You will get the glory from each party even those that are used by the enemy against You. Lord God, I thank You right now. It is in Your Son, Jesus' name that I ask these blessings, Amen.

An Upgrade of Your Faith
Hebrews 11:1-10

"Faith in Action."

"Now faith is confidence in what we hope for and assurance about what we do not see. This is what the ancients were commended for.

By faith we understand that the universe was formed at God's command, so that what is seen was not made out of what was visible.

By faith Abel brought God a better offering than Cain did. By faith he was commended as righteous, when God spoke well of his offerings. And by faith Abel still speaks, even though he is dead.

By faith Enoch was taken from this life, so that he did not experience death: "He could not be found, because God had taken him away." For before he was taken, he was commended as one who pleased God. And without faith it is impossible to please God, because anyone who comes to him must believe that he exists and that he rewards those who earnestly seek him.

By faith Noah, when warned about things not yet seen, in holy fear built an ark to save his family. By his faith he condemned the world and became heir of the righteousness that is in keeping with faith.

By faith Abraham, when called to go to a place he would later receive as his inheritance, obeyed and went, even though he did not know where he was going. By faith he made his home in the promised land like a stranger in a foreign country; he lived in tents, as did Isaac and Jacob, who were heirs with him of the same promise. For he was looking forward to the city with foundations, whose architect and builder is God."

Hebrews 11:1—10 (NIV)

Lord God, we thank You right now for the upgrading of our faith. We thank You right now for You putting us in position, and posturing us in such a position that You allow us to keep our faith toward You, moving toward You, ever creeping toward You, Lord God. We thank You that You help us move more swiftly, in a more faithful manner toward You, Lord God. We know that You are the Orchestrator for faith, Perfector of our faith, and You want to us to exhibit a faith that pleases Yo. So Lord God, we thank You right now, this day, with this fervent servant, this voice You have given, this heart You have given, this mind You have given. Lord God, thank You right now for putting us in a position to just take part in what You do and who You are, and how we love to serve You and be a part of everything that You have for us. In Jesus' name, we pray, and thank You for blessing those who hear this word. Amen.

3M research scientist Dr. Spencer Silver first developed a unique technology in 1968 while looking for ways to improve the acrylic— the acrylic adhesive that 3M uses in many of its tapes. But he found something remarkably different, and Dr. Silver did not know what to do with it. In 1983, the producer of many popular products which we use daily introduced the most popular which is a sticky note, more appropriately known as the Post-It Note.

Arthur Fry was fascinated with the technology Silver had stumbled upon because his bookmarks kept falling out of his church hymnal. Because of faith, teamwork, and the need to keep pages marked in that church hymnal, we have the Post-It Note. Imagine life without it. Not many people can, and at this point, we never will.

Let's consider the computer. There were predictions that there would never be more than three or four computers in the whole world, and now millions of us are walking around with them in the palm of our hand. Imagine the iPod. The Macintosh computer. Someone who was fired for inventing something and started a company in a garage of a college dorm room is now the richest man in the world, and recently passed away. People are very thankful for, Steve Jobs.

Ford. Now while I'm not necessarily a fan of Ford, they invented the automobile. All of these things happened because of our faith. And someone had to say, you're crazy. You cannot do it. I myself fall in that same category. Why do you keep publishing books if you're not already a bestseller? Or why do you keep publishing books if you haven't sold hundreds of thousands by now. Well, the answer is because God said to.

There was this man, who he had to be several hundred years old. He, his wife, his son, and a pair of every animal on creation got on this large boat called an ark. And because He put Noah and his family on this ark, God created the world again.

Understand that it is by faith that we move, not because of any other reason. It is by faith we move. It is by faith that we maintain our lives and a level of influence. It is by faith we are who we are, and what we eat. All of it is by faith.

When I decided that I was going to pursue education, it was by faith. It was a walk of faith that allowed me to do exactly what God said for me to do. The same with my publications, with my books, with my writings. I write and write and write for hours and hours, and then I type, and then I edit, and it is my faith that He's going to do the rest.

And so what we need to understand and ask ourselves is where does our faith land us? Where does our faith take us? Where does our faith keep us? And for all intents and purposes, we have to make sure that we are standing on our faith, because some days we are not.

So, let's look at the life of this upgrade and what happens in an upgrade of faith. Now, we always quote Hebrews 11:1 and Hebrews 11:6, but we never understand why those are very powerful scriptures. We look at them and we only really consider them as maybe some bookends, rather than the meat of the message.

When we talk about faith, and we use Abel as an example, we want to understand that Abel gave his gift to God anticipating nothing in return. Abel is our example because we need to offer our faith, our measure or worth, expecting nothing in return. Give who you are expecting nothing in return.

Now, I can't speak for you, but I can speak for myself, and there are times when I give things to God with an anticipation of a return. Like, a return on my investment, as if to say I am investing in stocks, and that is actually not true. When I talk about my investment, and what it is I've done, and what it is I do, I want to be able to say that I gave in faith regardless as to what was going to happen or take place. You have to give of yourself faithfully, of yourself, of your time, of your talent, of your energy, of your power, faithfully. In faith that, if He does something or nothing, you did what you were supposed to do.

Sometimes, He just wants to know that we will give, not how much, and not how often or how anything, it's just what we give. It is what we give. Are we holding something back? You see, some of us have this attitude of reserve; we always have to keep something in reserve. Well, that actually is not fair, that's not right. God doesn't hold anything back from us, yet we hold something back from Him.

So it's a period of time we have these conversations, when we talk, when we move about, we come in contact with faithless people. We hold things back from God; that is our lack of faith. How is that so? If you can't give Him what He's asked of you, and if you can't give it to Him with a hundred percent faith that whatever He does with it or not do with it is okay, then that's not faithful.

And what we're saying to God and to others? When we give that shabby offering as Cain did, we can expect those same results, and that was uncomfortable. We want to please God. And in that pleasing of God that means we've got to be obedient and give Him what it is that He has asked of us to do and to be.

We talk about Enoch and the fact that he was taken away so he would not experience death. Wow. And the reason was because he was someone who pleased God. And we have to ask ourselves— bring ourselves to the question: do we eagerly seek to please God on a daily basis? I can speak for myself again and I can definitely say not necessarily. Although I should, I do not necessarily seek to please God. I don't necessarily seek to say, let me see what I can do to please God today. Lord, what would it take to please You today? I don't seek that in my prayer time, I don't pursue that. So I want you to understand that when I consider that activity— when I consider that activity of being able to ask the question, 'Lord, what will it take to please You?': the Lord's going to answer me. If I say, 'Lord, what will it take to please you today?' He's going to answer me. And when He answers me, I'm going to have to do what it is He's asking of me. Plain and simple, that's how it is. That's what's going to have to happen. As a result of Him answering me, He's going to ask something of me, and when He asks it of me, I'm going to need to answer Him by doing what He asked of me.

And so when we also consider what pleases God, we have to consider who we are when we are pleasing Him. Selfless. Seeking the good of others. Seeking the good of those who are around us. When we seek that good, and when we seek that better way, we have no option but to please without any motives. Without any motives.

There was a series of four sermons and the ending sermon title was 'God gives through people whose motives are pure, and whose rights are relinquished.' That title stuck with me, because when you're talking about your motives being pure, and your rights being relinquished, you need to understand that we go into most everything with a "what's in it for me" attitude. What's in it for me? What do I get? If I do X for them, what is my Y going to look like? If I do Z, what is my A going to look like? If I do this, what am I going to get?

And in sales, we posture ourselves in a position to tell that to other people. We start out with, here's how it benefits you. We sell the benefits, we share the benefits. If it's a coffee machine, if it's a front door, if it's a wind chime, if it's a ramp, if it's a curb, if it's red paint: what are the benefits to the consumer? It's got to make a woman feel warm and fuzzy, for a man, it has to be practical. We have a sales pitch that is driven toward each individual. And so, with that being said, it's the same thing we do with God. That if I love my neighbor and myself, what's in it for me? If I have faith the size of a mustard seed, what's in it for me?

So at the end of every day ask yourself, what have we done to please God? And get out there and be bold and say, 'Lord, what can I do to show You my faith? A faith that will please You. What does it take to please You today?' We want to be sincere. Verse 6 says, "And without faith it is impossible to please God, because anyone who comes to Him must believe that He exists and that He rewards those who earnestly seek Him."

If you have children, there are times when your child will come to you asking you something, but believing that you're going to say no. They come, and you can tell on their posture, their face, their tone of voice, their rate of speech, that they believe that you're going to say no. They ask, waiting for the no. When you say yes, without that anticipation, and they walk away and they say, 'Okay, thanks.' 'Seriously? That is what you look like when I say yes.' Actually, they did not hear you because they were thinking you were going to say no. Sometimes we approach God in the very same manner. We believe He is going to say no, so we ask with the downtrodden, chin-to-the-chest voice, and expecting God to say no. Reflect on how do we approach God? How should we approach God?

When you consider the fact that He uses people He can trust to be faithful. When you consider Abel and Enoch, Noah and Abraham, Isaac and Jacob, He used people He could trust to be faithful. He uses people who do not quarrel intentionally. He uses people who do not whine because they did not get their way and that they are not being answered immediately. He uses those of us who He can believe that we're going to do what it is He says and stay faithful to the task up until completion. That's who He uses. Those are the people He can call on and ask, because we're going to please Him. He already knows our hearts are pointed due God. Our hearts are pointed toward him. They yearn and cultivated for Him, they're cultured for toward excellence for Him. And with that, we say, it is the heart that pleases God.

When God picked Noah to build and coordinate the ark nobody was thinking that this was a good idea, obviously. Noah was selected in Genesis chapter 5 because He can trust Noah. He couldn't trust the rest of us anymore.

Chapter 6 of Genesis, verse 5-9: "The LORD saw how great the wickedness of the human race had become on the earth, and that every inclination of the thoughts of the human heart was only evil all the time. [6] The LORD regretted that he had made human beings on the earth, and his heart was deeply troubled. [7] So the LORD said, "I will wipe from the face of the earth the human race I have created—and with them the animals, the birds and the creatures that move along the ground—for I regret that I have made them." [8] But Noah found favor in the eyes of the LORD." [9] This is the account of Noah and his family.

Noah was a righteous man, blameless among the people of his time, and he walked faithfully with God.

Verse 5-13: "So God said to Noah, "I am going to put an end to all people, for the earth is filled with violence because of them. I am surely going to destroy both them and the earth. So make yourself an ark of cypress wood; make rooms in it and coat it with pitch inside and out. This is how you are to build it: The ark is to be 450 feet long, 75 feet wide and 45 feet high. Make a roof for it, leaving below the roof an opening 18 inches high all around. Put a door in the side of the ark and make lower, middle and upper decks. I am going to bring floodwaters on the earth to destroy all life under the heavens, every creature that has the breath of life in it. Everything on earth will perish. But I will establish my covenant with you, and you will enter the ark—you and your sons and your wife and your sons' wives with you. You are to bring into the ark two of all living creatures, male and female, to keep them alive with you. Two of every kind of bird, of every kind of animal and of every kind of creature that moves along the ground will come to you to be kept alive. You are to take every kind of food that is to be eaten and store it away as food for you and for them. Noah did everything just as God commanded him."

He didn't get creative with the 450 feet by 75 feet by 45 feet. He didn't modify the directions. He did just what he was commanded to do. Noah wasn't a young man. Noah was six hundred years old when the floodwaters came on the earth. And it rained for forty days and forty nights.

Ask yourself, why was it that Noah was faithful enough and could be trusted enough to do just this— to do just what God had said to do? And that's what we have to ask ourselves: what am I doing that displeases God in such a fashion that I cannot be trusted with what it is He has for me? We've got to get ourselves focused on gaining His trust. That must take priority.

God is always telling us to go somewhere and do something. And my question for you is, when was the last time He told you to go somewhere and do something, and you did it at your convenience, your leisure, at your earliest opportunity, or you haven't yet gotten around to it? When we consider those activities, or we put down what God says on our to-do list, and we rank those numbers in order of what goes on the list last. Do you treat God's directions like that answering machine message, 'I will return your call in the order in which it was received.' But those things that God asked for come first. Part of us exercising our faith is to be able to put Him in priority, put Him at the top of the list. Putting His will at the top of the list. Of the things on my list, Lord, what can I do? What can I consider to be done? What can I consider that You want to take priority over what other thing? And so we have address this with God, we have to ask those things, because He is our God and our God alone. And if we do them out of order, then we can cause disruption in the plan, which we frequently do.

So when we upgrade our faith and consider what upgrade means, it is being invested in God at a high level, being able to understand, will He call us as one faithful servant? Or our behavior aligns with those who He commended as faithful, as pleasing Him? Is our attitude of right and righteous, what we want to please Him, and we seek to do that on a daily basis? And if we can't answer those questions in the affirmative then we've got to do some soul-searching and ask for some guidance from the almighty God. He will tell us what has gone wrong, if we seek Him and trust Him to do the same.

Lord God, how we thank You and love You. Thank You for sharing with us that we can upgrade our faith. But thank You for calling us into Your grace and mercy, even when we fail You in the faith area. But we thank You. We want to please You, Lord. Show me how to please You this day. Make You a priority, make what I do all about You, and make what You the wholeness of my agenda. Thank You, Lord God, for who You are and what it is You do in our lives. And just because You are Lord God, I thank You right now. In Your Son Jesus' name, I pray. Amen.

A Life Changing Walk
Matthew 14:22-36

Jesus Walks on the Water

²² Immediately Jesus made the disciples get into the boat and go on ahead of him to the other side, while he dismissed the crowd. ²³ After he had dismissed them, he went up on a mountainside by himself to pray. Later that night, he was there alone, ²⁴ and the boat was already a considerable distance from land, buffeted by the waves because the wind was against it.

²⁵ Shortly before dawn Jesus went out to them, walking on the lake. ²⁶ When the disciples saw him walking on the lake, they were terrified. "It is a ghost," they said, and cried out in fear.

²⁷ But Jesus immediately said to them: "Take courage! It is I. Do not be afraid."

²⁸ "Lord, if it is you," Peter replied, "tell me to come to you on the water."

²⁹ "Come," he said.

Then Peter got down out of the boat, walked on the water and came toward Jesus. ³⁰ But when he saw the wind, he was afraid and, beginning to sink, cried out, "Lord, save me!"

³¹ Immediately Jesus reached out his hand and caught him. "You of little faith," he said, "why did you doubt?"

³² And when they climbed into the boat, the wind died down. ³³ Then those who were in the boat worshiped him, saying, "Truly you are the Son of God."

³⁴ When they had crossed over, they landed at Gennesaret. ³⁵ And when the men of that place recognized Jesus, they sent word to all the surrounding country. People brought all their sick to him ³⁶ and begged him to let the sick just touch the edge of his cloak, and all who touched it were healed.

Matthew 14:22-36

We do not know a lot about Peter at this point. This is an introduction of who Peter is. As we understand who Peter later on in other verses, we get to know him as the man who would tell Jesus in Luke 8 that it is impossible to know who touched Your garment. Peter is the same man who denies Jesus three times although he said that he never would. This is the same man who as Jesus is being arrested cuts off the ear of the soldier. Jesus tells Peter that this is not the time for this behavior, places the ear back and heals the soldier. Peter initially rejected the foot washing. Peter is the same disciple who is sleeping during prayer. Peter is continually testing the boundaries, whether established or implied. He is always testing the limits and violating the limits that he chooses.

This introduction is when Peter challenges Jesus with, "If it is You, then call me out to You. Ask me to come out of the boat." How extravagant of a request is that by Peter? When we make these extravagant requests, we never actually anticipate the answer. Then Jesus says, "Come." One word. No explanation. No elaboration. He just says, "Come." After Jesus' statement, Peter thinks that he can follow these directions. Peter climbs out of the boat, he walks on the water, and he goes toward Jesus. Something very important happens in verse 30. Peter starts to look around. From what we know about Peter's character, it was probably rather arrogant, with an attitude of 'do you see me? Jesus invited me out here. Not you all. Just me. I just want to make sure that you see this.' But that looking around is when he got into trouble.

Let's examine the scripture background. Jesus has just fed the 5000 plus women and children before verse 22. Jesus wants to pray and so He sent them ahead. He finishes praying and goes out to join them. He does not need another boat. He is Jesus: He starts walking out to them. He does not need them to stop or even to slow down. They could have been in a motor boat. He is still Jesus and can catch up to them and He will catch up to them. Jesus can shorten the distance between He and thee anytime He decides.

As I studied these scriptures, which are some of my favorite, I wondered when Jesus realized how much power He really had, the type of authority He would be able to use, and how far is His reach stretched. When did He discover that power? When did He really realize that He was that powerful? That is what I want to know. I know when we realized it but when did He know? We realized it when His mother, Mary, asked Him to turn the water into wine.

I recently watched the movie, Man of Steel. The father of the young boy, who eventually becomes Superman, tells the son to not share his powers with anyone; do not do those things which bring attention to yourself. Do not let anyone know who you are and of what you are capable. There is an accident with a bus which it flips over a bridge. The boy is a passenger of the bus. The boy takes the whole bus to safety then goes back into the bus to get the driver. When the accident is resolved, the police are investigating and asks 'what happened?' There is silence, umms and uhhs. We cannot tell the truth about this situation. The father warned again that you cannot do that son.

But we never say that about Jesus. We never say to Jesus 'do not show off, do not do the miracle thing, do not turn water into wine, do not give the blind man his site, do not help the lame man walk, do not heal the women with the issue of blood, do not heal the woman with the 18 year disposition; do not do those things.'

When did Jesus realize that He could walk on the water?

The Courage from Jesus to Avoid the Consistent and Inappropriate Fear

We are consistently and inappropriately fearful, frightened, and afraid. The question which that begs, is why is that? Why is that? Why are we consistently fearful? We can be counted on for that behavior.

In verses 26, "It is a ghost," they said, and cried out in fear. In verse 27, But Jesus immediately said to them: "Take courage! It is I. Do not be afraid."
In verse 30, But when he saw the wind, Peter was afraid, and beginning to sink. It seems to me that if you are bold enough to request to be invited out on the water, the least you can do is to be bold enough to stand there. You were worried about the wrong thing. By the way, if I am in the boat and you are on the water and you begin to sink, I am going to talk about you when you return to the boat. We are going to have a misunderstanding. If you were bold enough to ask to go out there, He allowed you to challenge Him in this manner, and He allowed you to come out there, then you should not be afraid.

If you are bold enough to ask to be out on the water, in the wind, with Jesus, then why are you afraid?! That is the best you had to offer Christ? You offered Christ your fear? If that is what you had to offer Christ, you should have stayed in the boat. Stay in the boat! Next time let someone else go!

I know that Peter does not have the benefit of 2 Timothy 1:7, however Jesus led with, "Take courage! It is I. Do not be afraid." I am not sure how many minutes it takes between the vision of the Jesus to the challenge of Jesus to His invitation. I do not how long it takes to get out of the boat. I do not know how long it takes to walk to Jesus. I have no idea of the distance between Jesus and the boat. What concerns me is what is on your mind during this walk to Jesus that he arrived only to sink. The scripture said that he was toward Jesus, which means he has not made it quite yet. He begins to sink within a foot or two of reaching Jesus. But why should you be fearful and afraid and you are actually in the very presence of Jesus. They are actually in a boat in front of Jesus. He is right there!

When we decide to be fearful on a regular basis, my question is why does that happen and why do we think that behavior is acceptable. Jesus said do not be afraid. God did not give us the spirit of fear (2 Timothy 1:7). Who gave us that fear? Where does this fear come from? Better question is why do we keep it and hold on to it? Why are we holding it captive? Why are we holding on it like it is worth something? When in doubt, grab fear. That is unacceptable. That is not representative of the God we serve. This is not of the Jesus who turns water into wine and resurrects Lazarus from the dead. That is not representative of the Jesus who walks on water and invites us to do the same. Fear is not of God or Jesus.

How can we cast that fear out? We need to spend time casting that fear away from us. If you think that you are going to be fearful, then you should ask God to remove that fear and to be shown God's will so that we will have direction and release of the fear. We should not be afraid to ask to be relieved of our fears.

My son stakes his reputation on being a daredevil. He is not afraid of anything. If he could introduce himself to you this what he would: My name is Nehemiah and I am a daredevil. There was a t-shirt at the store which I should have purchased one in every size which reads: I do my own stunts. I could have kept him in one at every size. He would not have ever outgrown them until early teens. He does not understand the concept of fear. He could not wait until he was old enough and tall enough to ride the roller coasters at Fiesta Texas in San Antonio, Texas. He could not wait to learn to skateboard. He could not wait to play football. I know for sure that if I said come walk on water with me, he would try with me. If Mommy said we could walk on water, he would go with me. I would have to harness him without instilling fear within him. He currently wants to surf. I told him no. He looked at me with shock. I told him that I could not stop him as an adult, but from here to eighteen, I am in charge and the answer is no. The reason I told him no was because of something that happened to someone else. We do not make decision for fear of something will happen.

When we have evidence of something happening, we need to make decisions accordingly.

Recently, there was someone who went on vacation, on which he took surfing lessons. He came home paralyzed from a surfing lesson. He never enjoyed the waves and the adrenaline rush of the activity. He was not in the ocean irresponsibly. He did not come home the same. I said no. No surfing. This is not out of fear; this was out of making a good decision based on the possibility. Make good decisions not based on fear.

Let's return to Peter because he is often our example of what not to do. Not to sleep during prayer. Not to leave God. Not to misunderstand Jesus. Not to misunderstand your purpose for your time with God. Not to misappropriate our time with God. Peter does teach us some things.

The Challenge Peter Offers to Jesus

Let's talk about his challenging of Jesus. Verse 28 reads, ""Lord, if it is you," Peter replied, "tell me to come to you on the water."" We are learning about Peter. When Jesus led with "Do not be afraid, it is I," you actually had no need to question Him. Who else would say that? You should have recognized the voice of Jesus. He has been talking with you daily, providing instruction every day. If you just wanted to go out on the water, then just say, 'I want to come out there. Pick me. I want to go. We all want to come out.' Based on what Peter did, I am glad I was not there. I would have jumped out in front of Peter as he was exiting the boat. I would have been ready. I would have told Jesus that Peter could no longer make it.

There is a reason why I would have possibly behaved poorly: This is an awesome opportunity! You are walking on water with Jesus. This is an awesome opportunity which you have ruined with some fear. Peter led with 'if it is You.'

Peter introduces the doubt that he has. Peter is doubtful but if you have walked with Jesus any length of time, doubt should not exist. Peter should have been able to recognize His voice. Peter should have been able to recognize Jesus' voice with his eyes closed, in the dark, hands behind your back, blind-folded. When Jesus said, "It is I." There should have been no further doubt. They should have said, 'It is not a ghost. It is Jesus.' They should have said, "Jesus, do You need anything out there? Do we need to stop the boat?" No! None of them asked that. Instead Peter says, "Prove it to me!" Do we need any additional proof? We should not. Do we need any additional reasons? We should not. Yet, Peter is still asking, still questioning.

This challenge introduces the next challenge. What are you prepared to say to Jesus when you reach Him on the water? Our water is our daily walk. When we get out of bed every day, when we leave home, and when we get out of the car, we are walking on water. We are walking on water because we do not know what we will face, or what will be expected of us. Every one of us has driven our normal path only to face traffic, which we learn is the result of an accident. At that point, we praise the Lord because we consider the chances that we could have been involved if we had not left our coffee in the house or had a wardrobe malfunction, and had to go back in the house to correct another situation. Ten minutes late. That is a walk of faith on water.

When you are asking for big things, you want God-sized things to happen in your life, you want things beyond your imagination, then that is your walk on water. So you are challenging Jesus but you are unprepared to have this conversation with Jesus that should be imminent. Peter never had that conversation with Jesus. Now, they are walking on the water back to the boat. Peter has his head down trying to offer some feeble apology in this unfulfilled experience. Jesus is shaking His head in disbelief. The disciples are standing in the boat with their arms folded, thinking what I stated earlier, wishing they had asked to walk with Jesus and jumped out of the boat ahead of Peter.

We should recognize the opportunity for the walk of a lifetime. We should be prepared for the walk of a lifetime. It could happen at any time. We need to be prepared to share our testimony about our walk and the outcome.

The Comfort Jesus Offers

Verse 29 reads, "Come." In verse 30, "Peter cries out, "Lord, save me!" Verse 31 reads, "Immediately Jesus reached out His hand and caught him." Twice in the selected scriptures the word immediately is used. Verse 27 reads, "But Jesus immediately said to them," and verse 31 reads, "Immediately." Jesus does not let it tarry. He offers an immediate comfort, an immediate resolve, an immediate solution, an immediate remedy to your situation. You did not have to wonder what was going to happen. You did not have to check on the matter; it was handled. Immediately.

There are reasons why God responds immediately. Then there are reasons why He does delay His answer and response and action. Remember Job's answer was not immediate. In this situation, Peter's resolve was immediate. Maybe Jesus just needed to move Peter along. The subsequent events involving Peter would require His time and attention as well; time that He did not really have. Peter's actions will test all of Jesus' unlimited love and patience. Peter tries to use them up. Between cutting off the soldier's ear, denying Jesus three times and satan asking to sift Peter, Peter keeps Jesus busy but at the very worst of times.

So, Jesus is not going to save neither Peter nor us immediately, but today He chooses to save him immediately. It is His choice. We cannot ask, 'Jesus, why do not You save me like You saved Peter?' If you ask that, then do you want all the treatments of Peter? Do you want his whole testimony? We do not want the same weight and responsibilities of Peter, so we may not want Peter's privileges or favor. If you ask for his level of favor, then you are asking for his testimony as well.

How do you address God when you have doubted Him, yet He saves you? What do you say to God when you have doubted Him, questioned Him, and challenged Him, yet He saves you? What do you say? What is an appropriate conversation?

This sermon is titled A Life Changing Walk. I want us to have a life changing walk. Peter did not have the benefit of the rest of the Bible and teaching preachers. Peter does not have the benefit of this sermon. We have the benefit of Peter's opportunity gone awry. How is this different from Peter's situation though? Do we always recognize those walk on water moments? Do we always get it right when we are invited to walk on water.

We are invited to walk on water every day at God's invitation. God wakes us up daily. God breathes graciously on us daily. That is a walk on water. Do we make our days life changing?

Jesus asks Peter, "Why did you doubt Me, still?"

I have a question: What happen between the question and the return to the boat? My only visual of this includes Peter vowing silently that he is not going to say or do anything else. Peter cannot help himself though. In the next chapter, chapter 15, Peter asks Jesus to explain the parable. Jesus asks in response, "Are you still so dull?" Remember, this is Peter we are studying.

We keep waiting on proof of life. This becomes important because we want to see proof of God and Jesus showing up in your situation, in the image that you have preconceived and the image and the figment which you have made up, rather than the messenger which God chooses to send.

Jesus shows up to Saul, but God also calls Ananias to participate, to do the follow up. However, Ananias does not willingly participate. Jesus assures and reassures him that He is still in control. Ananias is debating with Jesus.

What does proof of life mean? In the movie, White House Down, they ask for proof of life regarding the President after he has been taken hostage. They cannot receive a picture. They only have proof of life based on the President's actions, his behaviors and what he has access to. There are people who are trying to take over the White House. Before the negotiations start, there needs to be undeniable proof that the President is actually alive. Those people do not have eyes in the room. All that they could depend on was the evidence in the room that his actions produced. Yet we question.

When God's hand is right there, we are asking, 'God, where are You?' God is sustaining that loved one when she has refused to eat and go to the doctor. God is holding your hand when you are receiving that bad news. Please do not attempt to imagine worse news than your bad news. So understand that He has already given you proof of who He really is and what He really capable of. God has given you sustainable, measurable, trackable proof of who He really is.

The problem we have is that we want to God to work like our corporate America education and experience. We want God to follow the SMART goals format. **S**pecific (simple, sensible, significant). **M**easurable (meaningful, motivating). **A**chievable (agreed, attainable). Relevant (reasonable, realistic and resourced, results-based). **T**ime bound (time-based, time limited, time/cost limited, timely, time-sensitive). God does not need to obey your education and rules.

God does not work on SMART goals. He works on God's goals. He works on His timing. Here is why. If He saves us immediately all of the time, we may forget it was Him. We won't have time to give Him the glory. We won't have time to realize and submit to God and say, 'Oh Lord, it was You! Oh my fault, I thought it was me.' You need to time to get from beside yourself. You need time to stop being full of thine ownself. You have to have time to give God some room to do His work. Those are the reasons why He cannot fix 'it' immediately. All of His actions and His moves are what makes the proof of life notion void and without credibility. There are times when you can reflect on what you wanted which was different than what God did and you were eternally grateful for God's intervention and the answer of 'no' to your prayer.

Back to my question, 'What would I say?' I keep wanting to answer that.

What does it take to discard our self-imposed fear? What are you going to do when God says come out on the water? This was not a question by the way. God did not say will you come. He said Come. This is a verb. This was a command with an understood pronoun of you. With an absolute period. You are not coming to satisfy God. He invited you to come in order to satisfy you. That is not what 'Come' was about. He did not need to prove who He was. He said, 'it is I.' He was walking on the water. His original intention was to get to the boat. So eventually He was going to arrive at the boat. Identity confirmed. So the Twelve of you would see Me together. Jesus thinks, 'But I am going to take this diversion with Peter.'

Maybe this story happened and Peter was used so that we could understand some things. Similar to your testimony. You go through things so that others can understand how God works and who God is. You and your testimony. You and your walk on water. You and the evidence He provides through you is the reason why these things happen is because you are proof of Life. You are proof that there is a God. You are proof that there is a Jesus. You are proof that there is a Holy Spirit. Are you using that appropriately? Are you really sharing your testimony with others? Are you sharing God with others? Or are you keeping it to yourself? That selfishness of withholding your testimony is cutting off the proof of Life.

Often people comment on how busy I am and that is true however, I evaluate if what I am doing advances God's agenda or my own. It is an exercise of obedience. Some of the things I am busy doing is an exercise of whether God can trust me and am I trusting Him based on what I asked for and what He is willing to trust me with. Some of those things are 'Are you going to trust Me and put your hand in My hand and walk through this thing together? You said that these are the things that you want so let's go. Are you willing to get out of the boat and walk on water toward Me in order to achieve and receive them?' 'Are you willing?' God asks.

When I hear parts of my testimony through introductions or others' evaluation, I am reminded of times when God has done such significant things in my life. There are times when I say, based on what I just survived and endured, I am good with this as my peak, attempting to ignore my future, but unable to do so. 'God, I am good with that.' God responds, 'No ma'am. I asked you to get out of the boat. I made provisions for you to walk on water. I ask you to walk toward Me. And as long as you have your eye on Me, then you won't sink.' This is a walk of faith. When you get out of your bed every day, that is faith. When you leave your home, that is faith. When you drive your car, that is faith.

What are we going to say when God says, 'Come.'? Why do we think it is okay to ignore Him? Why do we think it is okay to say no to God? We do ignore God. And make excuses.

God said, 'Daughter, apply for that job.' Your response was, 'God, that will take me across town and I do not want to be across town. I like it right here next to my house, where I work right now.' But you do not know who is at the new job which is designed for you to witness and who needs your testimony. You do not know who at that new job needs you to show them the God who has kept you looking amazing even though you should look unrecognizable because you have been through hell. You do not know who needs to see God because of your survival in spite of storm and circumstances.

You do not know that God can trust you with that situation when He cannot trust anyone else to go, so you are going to that new job. However, you do not know so you do not believe and you do not understand, so you do not apply for the job. You think, 'I am going to wait awhile before I apply.' And the job remains open. And you wonder why that is. But you finally apply. After taking your sweet time. Because you were being insolent. And disobedient. And then the job closes at the receipt of your application is received. Then you are looking around, then you look up. And you are perplexed. Still not able to acknowledge God for His sovereignty.

The Good News is that Peter did the right thing: Peter got out of the boat, walked on water, and came toward Jesus. That is what we are supposed to do. Our steps are to stay focused on Him who called us out of the boat. Do not look back. It is not time to text your friends. It is not time to call your mother. 'Mom, I just got of the boat.' No! Focus man, focus! We do not have time to be distracted. We are not watching television. This is not time to catch up on your favorite shows. Focus. You got out of the boat, which means you left your comfort zone. Focus on the One who called you out of the boat! Do not look down. Do not look around.

I just want to make a note here that you may have been invited out of the boat because you too asked a bold question. Go back and look at your prayer journal. What in your prayer journal is out of the norm? A bit above average? Without boundaries? Out of box? Extravagant? The stuff you have not told anyone? The stuff that you keep real secret? The stuff that you have not told anyone because you are afraid of what they are going to say to you?

Here is the question that I have: What are you prepared to say to Jesus when you are out there on the water? What are you going to say when you have His undivided attention? In a very strange place? Awesome disposition? Defied gravity? The laws of nature? What are you going to say to Jesus? Other than 'Wow and Whew, Lord'? What are you going to talk about other than, 'You got me out here Lord, now what?'

What are you going to say to Jesus to complete the experience? This is time to thank Him. This is the time to appreciate Him. This is the time to adore Him. This is the time to ask Jesus, 'How can I better serve You? What would You like me to do next?'

This experience with Jesus and Peter is never mentioned again. He never shares this with anyone else. He never discussed the feedback or lack thereof from the disciples. When He returned to the boat, verse 33 reads, '33 Then those who were in the boat worshiped Him, saying, "Truly You are the Son of God." Well, He had already proven that.

What are we going to say once outside of the boat? For every situation, your questions and answers may be different. But what are you telling God? What are you asking Him for? What are you sharing with God when you have His undivided attention, private time, on an awesome piece of land, in unchartered territory, defying gravity—what are you telling God? That is what is happening in your prayer life right? That is what is supposed to be happening in your prayer life—saying those things that are on your mind, that are truly things you all can share together. Let's do that going forward.

Jesus said, 'Come off the couch, out of the bed, out of your fog and walk into the places that God has already prepared for you.'

Amen.

A Good Definition of Nothing
Psalm 16:2; John 15:5; 1 Corinthians 13:2-3

O my soul, you have said to the Lord, 'You are my Lord, My goodness is nothing apart from You.'

Psalm 16:2 (NKJV)

"I am the vine, you are the branches. He who abides in Me, and I in him, bears much fruit; for without Me you can do nothing."

John 15:5 (NKJV)

"And though I have the gift of prophecy, and understand all mysteries and all knowledge, and though I have all faith, so that I could remove mountains, but have not love, I am nothing. And though I bestow all my goods to feed the poor, and though I give my body to be burned, but have not love, it profits me nothing."

1 Corinthians 13:2-3 (NKJV)

So for the time that we'll spend together today, we are going to talk about a good definition of nothing. I want to understand with you that nothing is defined as no things, as a void, emptiness, completely nothing. When you look at the void of the world and you look at what we do in the world, everything we are designed to do, everything that we are designed to work for and have, is based on something.

When we talk about wanting to get somewhere and be something, it is just all based on "something." And that something is going to give us what we need, and it is what we hang our hat on. It is our tangible assurance that what we have done is worth something. But these verses explain to us that we have nothing apart from Jesus Christ. Now, understand that in this nothing— I looked at nothing, and said, when I say nothing, do I really mean a complete and total 100% definition of nothing?

Well, let's consider what it is. Let's consider what it means. Given the fact that dozens have been told, in these academic environments, you aren't born to amount to anything, you're born to amount to nothing— they have basically been told that your presence is once again complete and total void. Your activities are going to amount to zero. That is when you say something about nothing: I am nothing.

But we have to ask ourselves, and be completely honest with ourselves, and say, so, who tells someone they're going to be nothing? What if we exactly said, well, in my mind's eye, we are going to reduce that person to zero. But when we say nothing, it is similar to if someone says, what's wrong, and you say, nothing. Nothing is wrong. Meaning everything is right. Technically, that is not true.

When you talk about the fact that nothing is equivalent also to a person of a little or no importance, something without quantity or magnitude, something that is trivial. And the adverb says that nothing is without respect or degree. The adjective is amounting to nothing, as in offering to prospect for satisfaction, advancement, or otherwise. So for something to be nothing, as I look at the definition, dictionary.com, there are nineteen definitions referring to nothing, including seven idioms.

So, understand that we have a situation where we have to consider what it is we mean when we say nothing. What did Jesus mean when He said nothing? So, here we go.

First of all, in 1 Corinthians 13 says, "But have not love, I am nothing." In order to be of some significance, be about something, I have to have love. And having love also translates into being loved. Doing love. Acting love. We confuse, or we think, that we are love, and if you ask another person, they may actually tell you that is not the case. If you really want to know the truth about that thing, ask other people, am I love? Do I show up in love? Do I look loving? Do I respond loving?

How do I move towards love? Well, First Corinthians 13 gives a litany of the definitions of how that definition of love has been formed. But the love, in its totality, is an exhibit of who you are to others, not just who you are to yourself or to your loved ones, people who already are in your circle. Who are you to the perfect stranger? Who are you to coworkers? And not when things are going well, and when things are going roughly? You have got to ask yourself if this particular point in time is a good time to go forward in deciding to pick a fork in the road because it looks as if the decision is clear. I go left to be nothing, or I go right to love. And that may have done more to show love, and I want to share love, I want to be love, and I want to act love, and I'm going to love— I'm going to do all those things, because at the end of the day, even if I give of myself, but I do not have love, I am nothing.

We cannot function without love. We cannot function without being the very essence of love. We cannot exhibit Jesus in any kind of fashion without showing forth His love. And we also want to depart from that and say we love— we want to speak truth in love. When you say things that tear another person down, that is not loving. If you want to really use your love, put your love in to action.

Attempt to give back some feedback to someone, criticize them, if you will, but then show them that in a loving fashion. Then undergird them, which comes with how we move forward. That is when you love them.

You do not just go and dump all of it on them and say what you did yesterday was just stupid. And walk off. First of all, you do not use the word stupid. It is a degrading term. What you do is you say, what you did yesterday could use a little work. Here's what I mean by that. I think that if you considered this way and approached it this way and gave it this information, then it would have been a more complete explanation of what you need to do to go forward.

When we are teaching our children, we have to design our instruction around enhancing their self-esteem and not letting them feel like they're going to be nothing. We talk to other people, we do not know what else is going on, so your words could be the very words that, are the straw that broke the camel's back.

A couple weeks ago we had an incident where someone, a child, a fourteen year old, killed his mother because he said that she was being too abusive. She was the straw that broke the camel's back. But whatever else was going on around his world, in his life, he was fourteen. And you think, well, how much trouble could they have? How much could there be? Between grades and peers and peer pressure related to clothes and all those types of things, how can we reach our teenagers with love? Words are very important. How we use them is very important.

The Bible says that your tongue is a two-edge sword. It can promote life and it can also consider death. We are called to use those words judiciously and love actively. Love is not a passive activity. Love is an active situation. When you say you really love, it should show up in your work, your deeds, and your behaviors. Your love should show up in that, as did Jesus' love. It was not a situation where Jesus loved us passively. It was not a situation where Jesus loved us passively.

There's that parable about the non-Biblical parable, and the parable about the egg, the ham, the chicken, and the pig. Well, the pig was committed to your Thanksgiving ham. The pig had to die for your meals. The chicken was just involved. The chicken laid those eggs and then laid more eggs. The chicken was a contributor; that is passive love. The pig was totally committed; that is active. Ask yourself, how actively are you involved in the love that you have for other people. Be it that you know them or not.

Without love, we are nothing. So, do a self-evaluation on your ability to love other people, even if those other people are people who you do not know and are not on your favorite's list. But sometimes we have got to get to a point where we love the unlovable, love the unloving. We love people who we do not necessarily like, and maybe who do not like us. We do not have a personal problem with them, but they do not gravitate toward us. And so, you cannot— this is not the tit-for-tat zone, I've said this many times. People get into that tit-for-tat, and next think you know, we have got a problem. So, understand that love is a proactive situation. Love is something we give away as the standard because God expects it of us and we expect it given to us.

Jesus gives us so many examples of His loving activity, between healing and forgiving, and after baptizing and saving our sorry souls, we have to definitely ensure that we are loving God appropriately, and loving God includes loving others. We cannot do one without the other, and we get so caught up in trying to make that right and make that work, but that is not an answer to the situation we find ourselves in.

Psalm 16 and first Corinthians 13:3 lets us know that our goodness is nothing apart from Him. A lot of times we want to frame our deeds up, and say, well,

I'm a good person. And you find people that are not in a relationship with Christ, they say this often as well. Well, I'm a good person. I feed the homeless. I am charitable. I give to the local community things. I give to kids. But I have no relationship with Christ. That doesn't profit you anything, those points, those markers that you're building up, mean nothing. But your relationship with Christ is the totality to everything. When you're in a relationship with Christ and you do those things, that is what's called your faithful service. That is a part of your service to Christ. And so we want to be clear that just because we do things that are good, apart from Jesus Christ, they mean nothing. Before your relationship with Jesus Christ started, all the things you did are not going to go toward your—if you want to call it—your Heaven credit. People get involved in that, well, I'm doing all this and I'm going to Heaven. That is not how you get to Heaven. That is not how your relationship to Heaven is formed or sustained, in any format. But even without Jesus my goodness means nothing. Part of it is because your goodness gives you glory. But the goodness you're to get out of the relationship with Christ, you give it to God.

One of my favorite songs by Pamela Mann, "Take Me to the King," says, I'm going to put my crown at Your feet so You get all the glory. If I have on the crown, someone's going to give glory to me. But I owe all of my glory and honor to God. If I put my crown at His feet, He'll get all the glory. And we have to remind ourselves of that. It is not for us that we live, but it is in order to serve Him through us that we are designed to be here. Our designation needs to be made clear and firm. That is why we are designed to be here.

You have got to make sure and clear that you understand it is designed for you to be here. We do not have time to talk about design today, in this format, however part of why we are designed to be here is our attachment to Jesus Christ. That is 99% of it. Everything else is designed to do with that 1%.

Now, we have to remember to stop doing things for selfish motives. If you're not going to give Christ the glory, if you're not going to give Christ the credit, then you have done it for selfish gain. You have done it for personal profit. And in the long run that personal profit is not going to profit you at all. We have got to be leery of that, we have got to be careful of that scenario. We do not want to get caught up into keeping doing things just for self.

When we consider John 15, "I am the vine, you are the branches. He who abides in Me, and I in him, bears much fruit; for without Me you can do nothing." The beginning of that chapter discusses that God is the Vinedresser. He is the Gardener. He prunes back parts of us that are not healthy, and that are not whole, and are not bearing the type of fruit that He designed us to have. And so He talks about how you bear fruit, which is this verse right here. "He who abides in Me, and I in him." There's a mutual relationship here. I've got to abide in Christ and Christ is going to abide in me. Because without Christ I can do nothing. The things I put in my hand will not yield any fruit apart from God.

I am not a gardener. I have no green thumb to speak of, but I do know a little bit about plants, and planting trees. Trees are seasonal. You apply fertilizer, food, water, and sunlight. And that is the prescriptive measure to foster growth in a tree or a plant or flower.

When you go to the nursery and buy these items to plant them at your home or backyard, you look at the tag. The tag tells you, this particular plant or tree likes direct sunlight, needs lots of shade, needs food three times a week, and do not overwater. It gives you some specific instructions on how to nurture this tree or this plant to a healthy life. Well, that is the same thing we have here with the word of God and Jesus Christ. That relationship with God and Jesus to foster growth within us, where He profits and we reap benefits from the residual effects. We have to call ourselves into a relationship and an understanding of what we have already been called to. God calls us to draw near to him. He's waiting on us to answer to Him. And once we are in a relationship, that is not the end of the call of the drawing near. He calls us daily to draw near to Him through prayer, meditation, supplication, and quiet time. He calls daily to that, because daily we need to focus on Him. Daily.

We make these lists of things we want to do: our goals, our dreams, or desires. We make those types of lists, we do. And what we want to realize is that none of those things are going to come to come to fruition the way you would have them to, if He is not the author and the originator of them under His will. We want to do a whole lot of things, but until it is His will, those things will not come to pass.

'Well, Onedia, you know there's people that do not have a relationship with Christ; they get everything they want. They get things they want all the time. How is that possible?' I understand your point. But do they have joy? Are they always searching for something? It is the emptiness that they have within that you do not have. This joy that I have, the world did not give it, and the world cannot take it away. I call those things that they have their life-preserver, because they feel like without those things they have no life.

So one of the things we need to realize is that I can do nothing without God. The things I want to do are going to be nothing without God. Nothing without God.

Now, understand something. We have been told without Him we can do nothing. Apart from Him we can do nothing. And without love in Him, we can do and be or profit nothing. So what are we saying? Here's a question— you know I always have a few.

So with Me, capital M, Jesus Christ, you can do everything. Yes. According to My will.

Living A Whole Life

Who are you without Me? Nobody, and nothing.

And if I could lift the words out properly, He would also say, "You did not create yourself and did not give yourself life. You did not save yourself. Without Me, none of these things transpire. So be careful when you boast and pat yourself on the back for something you did not do."

So what will you do without Me? A capital M. And the answer is nothing.

And understand that it is the acknowledgement of Him, the relationship with Him, that we are without. I personally believe that God does not let even those people that are not in a relationship go without Him, go without His will. I think that they go without a relationship with Him, but they they're still under God's umbrella. He's the creator of everything, of everyone. He certainly did not create a bunch of nobodies and do-nothings. He wants that relationship to happen.

Who are you without Me? If He asks me that question, who are you without Me, and why are you trying to function and live without Me? And that is a great question. I like that question: why are you trying to live without Christ? Why are you trying to omit Him from your daily walk, your daily doings, your daily talk? And I'm talking to believers now; I'm not talking to non-churchgoers or non-believers. I'm talking to us who are Christians 'saved, sanctified, and filled with the Holy Ghost' isn't that what we say. 'Blessed and highly favored,' that is what we talk about? Who are we, trying to function and live without Him? Why do we do that?

If you look back over the time in your life, starting with today and yesterday, that you tried to function and live without Him, you tried to do some things without Him. You wanted to do it on your own. 'I've got this; I do not need God for these things.' But is that true? Is that the case? Is that really how you feel about it? Is that really how you feel about it?

When we attempt to function without Him, it is like we are swimming along and then the current pulls us down, and then we start flapping our arms, and treading water, and screaming for help. And at the same time, we are seeing ourselves sink. We are wonder why He won't reach in and save us immediately. But it is because we are functioning without Him. In order to not drown and fall into the abyss, we have got to turn those things over to Him—everything—and let Him handle it.

Exodus chapter 14, verse 14 reads: The Lord fight my battles if I would just be still. We do not want to do that. Even if He puts us before the battle line, Ephesians chapter 6, verses 10 through 18, we still need to put on the armor. We leave home without it. We leave all our armor at the armory repair place; we don't ask for a new equipment pack, we are going to ask for a replacement pack, but you cannot just go out there naked. Without our armor, naïve to the enemy's attack. Confused as to what's going on, and then wondering, what happened, God? Oblivious, in the abyss.

So when we consider who we are and what God has designed us to do, without Him, it is the definition of nothing. It is going to supersede, but a good definition of nothing would be you to tether yourself to God. A God who loves you and wants to save you, wants you to serve Him.

I thank You for forgiving me of my sins, and I thank You for expanding my territory, Lord God, with my books. Thank You for allowing me to publish number thirty-seven. Lord God, I thank You right now that You are blessing and whatever it is You would have me to do. So, Lord I thank You for allowing me to just serve You and serve You in a healthy manner. It is in your Son Jesus' name that I pray and ask this blessing. Amen.

That You Might Endure
James 1:2-4

Trials and Temptations

² Consider it pure joy, my brothers and sisters, whenever you face trials of many kinds, ³ because you know that the testing of your faith produces perseverance. ⁴ Let perseverance finish its work so that you may be mature and complete, not lacking anything.

James 1:2-4

When you consider the definition of endurance and for that matter, perseverance, you want to consider, who uses perseverance and endurance the most? Let us consider runners.

The marathon is 26.2 miles, and this marathon is something that is a highly coveted award of being able to run, and complete. There are great lengths of preparation that go into this process. Those who are training for the marathon run daily. They have certain diets that they consume. They have certain methods in which they manage their consumption of goods. They have things that they do that are special during this training and designed just because they are going to be in a long, arduous race. Continuing to do these types of exercises does something to condition your heart. The exercise conditions your heart in such a fashion that you are able to run for long periods of time and not get tired quickly.

In this preparation period, you are working to make sure that you are able to run the entire race. That is your goal so you build up your stamina for the entire race. You practice regularly. In addition to practice, you are going to manage your diet: what you take into your body; you are going to manage your time: how long does it take to run this marathon? How many days of training does it take for you to run the entire marathon? In order to prepare for a marathon, you have to run the length of the marathon several times to make sure that you are able to finish the race.

So the difficulty that some of us have is exposed. Now, I am not a runner. I do not profess to want to be a runner. I do not want to run that far or that long. I do not want to be a professional runner. I do not want to run a marathon. I do not want to have that claim, but many do, and it becomes a moment of prestige to say that you have completed a marathon. People get excited because what that means is you are a finisher. When you say you have run a marathon, you are a finisher of something that requires endurance, practice, length of time, and involves intense training. Anyone who has finished a marathon is going to regard you highly when they hear that you have finished your own marathon, your first marathon, or some version of the marathon. They are going to be impressed to the level that they want to talk to you about that experience. They want to find out if you have covered the same milestones they have covered. They want to know if you have achieved the same things they have achieved when they did their marathon. When you are sharing at a dinner party or a social event, you are speaking a different language than others in the room.

When we are developing this perseverance, this endurance to run this race, and we compare that to the life that we lead, on a daily basis, we want to understand that we are going to encounter some pitfalls, likewise the runner does that very same thing: runs into some pitfalls, run into some challenges in their training; they may get ill, or get hurt, busy at work, project with their kids and these issues puts the runner off schedule. A part of the completion of the whole process is part of the endurance that is necessary to maintain the focus on running the marathon.

WE ARE IN A RACE

We are in a race! This race called life is not for the faint hearted. This is a race which involves endurance; this life requires perseverance. A race of life, it involves doing things that you had not signed up for, commitments which you did not remember, for activities which you did not realize that you would be responsible for. So it involves those types of details which you are going to have to prepare yourself for with that same caliber of excellence, you have prepare, practice, and perform the things that matter most.

As you consider this race and those things that are a part of this race, as we consider what equips us for this race, we are going to realize that we are designed for this race and to be the best us that we can be.

I TEST YOU SO THAT I WILL I KNOW YOU

Our first point today is "I test you because I have to know you and your reaction is important to My name." God tests us so that He can know us, and so that we can know ourselves. Our reactions are important to His name. When I say reactions, our response to the things that we are designed to endure is important to who God is. God cannot get the glory when we are quitting and we are looking around and trying to figure out what to do, when we are already equipped to complete the assignment. He can only get glory when we are doing what we are designed to do, and doing it at the time that we are designed to get it done, and doing it with speed and pace that He designed for us to get it done, that we might endure.

We have to get ourselves to a point where we not only endure but we endure at a level that brings Him glory. When He tests us that we might endure, we want to be able to be clear that we need to know ourselves and He is doing some of this so we can be introduced to this part of us, that we were completely unfamiliar with. In essence, what would we do when things like this happen, what would we do when things like that happen, what would we do when we are not prepared for what to do, so what are we going to do and who are we going to turn to, how are we going to respond, what is going to take place and when we get the answer to those questions then we are going to be able to say that we might endure, so here we go. When you talk about the things that you have experienced in your life versus the things you have accomplished, you did not accomplish without effort and some trouble, you talk about those things, you had to go through some things to get to that point. You had to go through some things to be at the level that you are, you did not just leave your mother's womb and walk; that did not happen.

We have to be trained to do the things we need to do, we have to be trained to walk, we have to be coached and trained to talk, to understand what it is we are designed to do. So likewise, for those things that God wants us to accomplish and achieve we have to be tested and trained to know how to do the right thing and how to do it well and do that well at all times, He tests us that we might endure. Again that endurance means that we do not quit, and that we are going to have a positive attitude. You cannot take the position of: 'I do not want to do it. I'm just going to quit. It just does not mean anything to me,' because that actually is not true. Technically, you want everything you set out for, you take action on everything important to you, you want to make sure you do everything you are supposed to be doing, and as God called and designed you to do. Otherwise, first, you will repeat the lesson, and secondly, you are going to disappoint our God; this causes us the potential to make Him look foolish. This behavior causes questions to come in regard to God, which are designed to cause someone to question God such as "If you are His child, should these things be happening to you?" That is true, and certain things that happen to you are because we are off course and off track, we are doing something we have no business doing and doing something improperly and with whom we should not be doing it, so we have to discipline and regulate ourselves, which means we will endure some things. We will go through some tests. We will endure some trials. There are things that we have to see in order to figure that out and those things are only going to happen by the test that we endure. We have got to build up our stamina for dealing with some of those events and activities.

The first time you find out that everyone does not love you, you are typically a child. I know some children in my life, namely my own, who do not understand when people do not love them. They know and believe and feel that everyone should love them, and that is true. We are commanded to love. God says that we are to love one another. The interesting is they know when people do not love them and so do we. Love carries energy and is a force which cannot be confused with other verbs or energy, nor can be replaced by other unsuitable substitutes. We are created to love everyone. I recently saw a billboard where the billboard would suggest based on scripture that read, "That 'love thy neighbor thing,' I meant that. God." Seeing a billboard which read that, which God obviously did not put up Himself, however called and equipped someone else to do so and they were obedient. They paid for that posting. Such a profound statement and such a profound movement of faith. The point is that God did really mean that. What He told us, He really meant; what God said He really meant; what God did He really meant.

Likewise, God is waiting for us to do what He said and carry out what He meant. He expects us to be the disciples which He called who can be trusted to do what He commands. God has commanded us to do some things and be some people who others have boldly rejected. He answers our prayers and places us in positions to achieve our dreams and accomplish the desires of our hearts. He is waiting on us to do what He says and really meant, and we need to do all of that. We have to get to that point where we can say and do what we are really supposed to be doing and saying and to follow God's directions as He intended.

Now, when we go through this test and discover our reaction, our first reaction cannot be which has previously been the case, 'I quit.' Now again understand the test is not fair. I know what you are thinking, and that is what you are saying: 'it is just not fair. Why can't I quit? Why can't I give up? Why can't I change course?'

When God tests you, it is not optional. This is not something you can opt into or out of, because you want to or desire to. It is not anything possible because these tests are not designed by you but for you; they were designed for you, but not by you. You cannot quit. You cannot give up. You cannot take a vacation. You cannot go on hiatus. You cannot do any of that because that is not the plan for you. You have to stay the course—you cannot quit. You have to go forward— you cannot stop. You have to be focused. You cannot get side tracked or frustrated. You cannot get off course by what is planned and what is being planned for you.

Understand that your reaction while others are watching you, is very critical because you are responsible for that information which they witness from your experience. This shapes their testimony. You are responsible for passing that test, you are responsible for progressing to the next level. While this is not technically like school, remember those people in school who failed classes, or grades, or fail things, we were all looking around saying 'how did that happen.' Well it is because it is true, it happened and it should not have happened. A little extra work every day will get you to a passing grade. I'm a teacher. I'm a proponent of it.

I also know that a little extra time with God everyday will keep us from failing and faltering, and that is very important in our Christian lives. That is what we are trying to not to do: fail or falter, so we have to be careful. We have to measure our time that we spend with God and practice our reaction, and our performance. We have to practice, just like the runner does to increase our endurance.

I TEST YOU BECAUSE I NEED TO KNOW WHO YOU ARE BECAUSE OF MY NAME

God created us. He is our Creator. There is no misunderstanding about that. He is the Author and the Finisher of my faith. I believe that, but I also know that some things we have done have separated us from the factory settings, so we have to do some new testing to understand our name. We have abandoned the name that He has put upon on us, and the names that we are supposed to be a part of and the name we are responsible to. We have gotten away from the very image that He created. We treat our image very differently than it is supposed to be treated. We treat it very flippantly; we treat it very poorly. It is very hard to get it back to the faith we are supposed to be professing, very difficult get back to that level of peace that He designed for us initially.

He tests us to know who we are because of His name. What are other people going to see when we are tested? What are other people going to say when we are tested? Is what we are enduring and surviving going to help other people to understand who God is? They cannot see what God is doing through us if we are quitting, and behaving poorly during our tests.

During the NBA finals, one of the team's players flopped to draw the foul. That was seen as poor sportsmanship and because of that the league fined him five thousand dollars. As a result, he's looked poorly upon in the league because of those types of behaviors.

When you build a reputation for flopping in your life, when you want to just quit, and fall out every time something gets tough, or difficult; every time something gets hard, or strenuous; every time something tests your faith and comes up against you to test that you really are a child of God, and you really do believe in His name and you do understand His love, grace, mercy and forgiveness, you make God look bad when you plan to quit. When you want to flop out and play like all is not well, then you put the back of your hand on your forehead and say, "Oh woe is me," as if nobody else is having trouble, or nobody else is having issues, or nobody else is in these tests that they might also endure, that you might also endure together, but you look at it as if you're the only one and He just picked on you. And why you?

And why not you? You're just good as anybody else to test because you still belong to God. You claim Him, His glory, you accept His gifts, His mercy, His love, the breath of life, your breathing every day, so it seems to me that you want to respond appropriately. Now likewise we want to understand ourselves, when I say that he tests you that you might endure, that He tests you that you so that you can understand the reaction, because that reaction will reflect on His name and that you want to be able to be clear about what that name means and what that name represents, and how you factor into that representation.

'I want to give you with a test because I need to know that you will endure the rest of the work I have for you.' You were put here with a purpose, Jeremiah 29:11: For I know the plans I have for you. Those plans are purposed, all driven back to give God glory. There's no way around that scenario, it has to be done that way. He's not going to allow you to not live according to your purpose. Not even you can stand in your own way. It is impossible and detrimentally so, should it take place. I believe with all of who I am that we need to be focused on what it is exactly God wants from us at all times, and with that we are going to have to go through some things in order to know and get to the next level. Allot of us like to tread water, if you will, get complacent, move around in the instance where we do not function at a level of challenge. Because we do not do that, because we do not get to that level, we have no drive. Well, that is not how He designed us. He designed us with an ample drive to accomplish whatever it is He designed for us to do. Now yes, we are going to ask what does He want me to do, what has God called me to do, and what does God have for me.

At the end of the day, there are some basic things we do not have to stumble on, or stammer over to figure out: one is to love ourselves, to love Him with all our heart, mind and soul, and to love our neighbor as ourselves. And that is why I said, and I said it out of order but I meant what I said when I said to love yourself. It takes allot to understand how to love yourself and we cannot spend any time on that because we need to stay on topic, but that is the whole point of our purpose of study, so it shows that our workmanship approved, and since He's created us for what He's planned in advance, Ephesians 2:8-10. We have things to do and purposed to do, and those things that are happening in your life should be lining up with the will of God and if they're not, then we need to reassess what we are doing because we need to be in line with the will of God. If we are not in line with His will, or we are going to keep having some issues that we currently have and nobody wants to do that.

Back to our endurance and our perseverance. In this life there are things that we have to do and there things we need to work through and work on, things we need to meld together and get focused on. We need to be better believers. We need to be better stewards over those beliefs. We need to be better managers of what we are responsible for and likewise what that means is that we need to be able to get to a point and to a place where we figure out that these tests are designed to help us build our endurance and perseverance through things that are going to come in our life. While we are in preparation, we cannot quit. Because if we quit, those things are not going to stop or be put on hold because we are not ready. They're going to come and we are going to be unprepared and taken by storm. We are going to be not ready and then we will blame God for our situations. Is that the truth? Is it His fault? We act as if it is optional to follow Him and do what He says, it is not.

As a resident of Texas, we have been through many storms, hurricanes, tropical storms, many weather related events which cause flooding. The storms that have progressively gotten worse for various reasons but during those storms getting progressively worse, we take note, every time something happens, that we are going to know that this time we learned a lesson so next time we are going to take that new information into consideration.

Hurricane Katrina made land fall in New Orleans, Louisiana, causing millions, or even billions of dollars worth of damage, but the important thing is that it gave people a lesson on how to evacuate. Hurricane Katrina and Hurricane Rita were in the same hurricane season, so Hurricane Rita caused Houstonians to evacuate and to go north or west. Well, in the escape route of the evacuation, we were taught another lesson and that lesson was that we would meet to figure out how to get out of town a little differently, have gas reserves a little differently, because we had got into a situation where we got that all together. Then realized we needed to get out of town differently, we ran out of gas, and had a medical emergency. People could not get out of town quickly due to traffic. We created an emergency response team as a city, developed a plan on how we would evacuate from said storms. Understand that we are always on the preparing to be ready for the next thing. Likewise, God would have it no differently. God wants us to understand what He wants us to be able to do at any given time and we do not have any idea how we are going to use this information that we are gathering or the things we are going through. All we need to know is that we need them eventually.

There's this old saying that 'I'd rather have it and not need it than to need it and not have it.' In that situation you have got to ask yourself if I have it and I do not need it, that is one thing. If I need it and do not have it, what is it going to cost for me to get it, is it going to cost me my life, is it going to cost me money, my time, what is it going to cost to be prepared for what God has for me. Understand you have got to get yourself in a preparation mode that says I'm going to be ready for whatever God calls on me to do. In order for that to happen, you have to be engaged on a daily basis, and on the ready for what he has for you, so whatever that looks like, we have got to do it so there's no complaining, no whining, no crying, no putting your hand down, no quitting, no taking a break. You have got to stay in the fight every day. satan doesn't take a break, how can we?

Instead of saying 'I need rest and just cannot get it together,' you might want to suck it up, and get past that point because there's this man I know of and He did not quit. He carried a cross up a hill, and then they put Him on that same cross and then they pierced Him in His side and put nails in His hands but He did not get down from His cross, and because He did not get down of that cross, I do not get the right to quit. He did not get down off that cross and He could have easily quit. He asked for this cup to be taken from Him but then said, 'not My will, but Thy will be done'.

We have to remind ourselves this is just a test. I know you might not have seen it in many years and neither have I, but I remember there was these multi-colored vertical bars, that was made up of color pattern across the screen and about 3:30 AM and at other various times of the day, there was a horn noise which introduces this message: 'this is test of the emergency broadcasting. This is only a test. If there was a true emergency in your area, this test will be followed by information and instructions on what to do next, but this is only a test of the emergency broadcasting system.' That means that you have got to endure some things.

You're not going to just get into everything handed to you, and it is not going to just be put in your lap, not going to be a situation where you just easily receive every single time what you desire. You have got to endure and the more you endure, the better your endurance becomes. You can go through storms for longer periods of time. Does that mean that God is going to test me for a longer period of time? I do not know that, but God is God and can do whatever He chooses. He knows what's coming and He knows what the test is going to look like, and He knows what you need to endure. He knows only the people who'll come to talk to you, which are going to need information that only you have; He knows all of that.

Understand that at the end of every day, we have to guard ourselves against that desire to quit. So I want to just implore you to get into your mode of great endurance. It is what you did when you finished high school, college and any additional education. It is what you did when you finished that program. It is what you did at the end of that illness. When you were recovered, fully healed and back to health and the doctor said that you will never get out of this bed, but you got on the floor and walked again. It is those things, that you might endure.

Amen.

Father God, we thank You right now for what You have done in our lives, and we thank You for this word that You have sent, through Your vessel today. Lord God, we thank You for now for those lives that were touched. Thank You for reminding me that is the reason why You do what it is You do because You are God, our sovereign God. You love me. You take care of me. You have forsaken me for none other, and Lord God, I thank You right now because You do not let me stand on my own for the things You have for me, and that I might endure, the things You have going on in my life. Lord God, I thank You right now that this is not too hard for me, and it is something You said, that You will not give me more than I can bare, so I can bare more. You have given me more, you're training me. Lord, I thank You for that training. I thank You for that investment. I thank You for Your love of me Lord God. I thank You for being gracious and allowing You Son to die and be resurrected as the savior of my sins. I ask You to provide blessings over our lives in Your Son, Jesus' name I pray. Amen.

It is My Day to Watch Them
Genesis 4:9

⁹ Then the LORD said to Cain, "Where is your brother Abel?"

"I do not know," he replied. "Am I my brother's keeper?"
Genesis 4:9 (NIV)

It is my day to watch them. The story that this scripture has lifted out is the story of Cain and Abel. Cain and Abel are the children of Adam and Eve. The first people put on this earth. And with this story, Cain is upset because the Lord found favor in Abel's offerings but did not find favor in Cain's offerings.

The scripture says that because he is angry, instead of dealing with the person he is angry with, he deals with the person with whom he is jealous of. And so he is jealous with Abel's favor with the Lord because of his gift. Now, having that back story, understand that the Lord says that Cain's sin caused him punishment. Likewise Abel's blood caused the loss on the ground and the ground opened up and accepted Abel's blood. And so in the scripture text, the Lord talked directly to Cain and said, 'where is your brother Abel,' and he says, 'I do not know; am I my brother's keeper?' When you lift that out of the paragraph, out of the scripture text, you won't understand that when the Lord came and saw Cain, looking for Abel, a number of things took place.

Number one, He wants to know whether really Cain would confess that really this is what you have done to your own brother. And then Cain decided to share his lack of regard or respect for the Lord by asking Him, 'am I responsible for him?' Well, all around the world the answer would be yes, yes you are responsible for your brother. And as a matter of fact, you are the oldest and all of that should not have taken place.

The Lord, now in dealing with him, related to, if you have done right, your world would have been favorable, but instead of doing right, he decides to do even more wrong. So let's look at what the scripture takes for teaching us today. Understand that the first thing, God asks, "Where is your brother?" The question that He has for us is where are the people that belong to you, and what is going on with them? The people that are around us are people who belong to us, we need to do is act like it.

Let's define who belongs to us, first, your parents, your grandparents, your immediate family, sisters, brothers, in-laws, extended families, cousins, uncles, nephews, even extended beyond the families, step-mothers, step-brother, step-sister, all the people that are around you belong to you. And when I say belong to you, you are responsible for them. Part of my point is the people around you belong to you, we need to act like it. By act like it, I mean there is a way we need to treat the people who belong to us. We treat them with kindness and care, we treat them with love, with respect, regard, and we treat them like they belong to us. You see, I know for a fact that some friends of mine, people very close to me wash their cars on a weekly basis. They detail it out, they made sure that it is dust free, dirt free, clean, speaking of it, you can eat your dinner off of their floor boards. Because the car belongs to them, it feels like as far as the car is the one they drive, they want it clean, etc.

Conversely, we should not treat people who belong to us like the dirt we just vacuumed out of our automobile. Why does that happen? Number one, why is it and why is it okay, why do you feel that is fine to do? When we mistreat these individuals, are we really saying to God, we love you, the answer is no. What do we need to do to treat them better? Why are we mistreating them? Just because you are upset with another person does not give you creative license or the authoritative license to treat them in your own way. So we need to act like it, we are responsible for those individuals. What do you mean, what does that have to do with me? It has absolutely everything to do with you. It has something to do with where they are, what they are doing, what they have, what they have access to and why, just why, why do they have these limitations? Why? Just why, where are they, what are they doing, and what they are doing, you are responsible for. For as it is now, you may not understand and say it is not fair. I understand, it might not be fair, but it wasn't fair for Christ who died for all of us either, but He did, so let's leave fair out of it for a while until we can get to a point where we can understand why and really understand that is the situation. So here is what I need you to understand. Number one, we can hold each other accountable even though we are responsible for one another. That doesn't mean that your sister can just get away with anything and its okay; that is not the case.

Now, we are going to leave out families, where mom lets the brothers and sister get away with everything that she doesn't let you get away with anything, we are going to leave them out, that is not the group we are dealing with today.

We are dealing with a group of people who are reasonable persons. But here is where we are heading, you have to know that you are responsible for their lives: your brother, sister, cousin Dad, you are responsible for those persons, where are they? And what are they doing and if you do not know, why do not you know? Why do not you know where they are? We have to put ourselves in a position where we can get to our families and do the things that we are called on for our families and for our friends at very high level, offering excellence, managing it correctly, managing our relationship properly at all times. Sometimes we feel like it is optional and it is not. So why am I responsible? Why do they belong to me? Why do I have to manage them? Why do I have to act like they belong to me? It is because that is your job and your job was given to you by God. When He gave us parents and siblings and others, He asked us to be a family. Family hold each other accountable. Family stays together. Family assists, likewise our friends.

To use Jesus as our guide, Jesus treats us like His friends, He says there is no greater love than this for a man to lay down his life for his friend. He treats us and sees us as friends, so likewise, He wants us to treat others the same way and that is not negotiable. While it may not make any sense to you, while it may be not fair, it is critical that we follow His directions. So we have to act like Him. There may be a time that we fall out. We have to make up for that; we are going to be held accountable to make up for that. We are going to be held accountable to make all relationships correct, make them right.

'Well, it was not my fault. I did not do that. That wasn't me.' I understand, but you are still accountable. And the fact that you know that you are accountable and do not want to be is altogether a different infraction, so we have to act like it. Acting like it means that we will respond accordingly. You are going to know where they are and you are going to know what they need and you are going to be responsible to help them and assist them in finding the resources to get this taken care of. The point is we are made to help each other.

It had been a while since I've seen my nephew so recently when I saw him, I asked him how he was and what was going on and how was everything going around and if he is well. He mentioned to me that he was looking for a job. And I said, 'okay. What kind of work are you looking for? What would you like to be able to do? What industry would you like to be in?' We had some more communication. Now, I could have left it right there; I could have said, 'well that is nice' and forged ahead. But what I started doing was calling my friends asking questions such as: 'are you hiring where you are, what is the application status where you are, what can you do for this gentleman where you are.' I started making connections; I started helping him. I stand to gain directly nothing, but indirectly I stand to gain everything.

You see, God gave me those types of resources in order to be helpful, when he said to me that he needed, he needed the person who could help him by picking up the phone and make some things happen on his behalf. In fact, it was my job to help him. Regardless of when it was really the last time I spoke with him or spent time with him, or whatever the reason of what had transpired, he still belongs to me. I will benefit indirectly because he will be employed, while he is employed, he is able to take care of his child and the child's mother. He will feel better about himself, so he will not be compelled to sin or do other things for resources. So it is my day to watch him.

You do not understand what it takes for a person to ask you for assistance or present themselves in a position of need. When you figure out what it costs them to say I need your help, and then you act as though you are not able to help them, what have you done? You have gotten on the side of satan. 'You just made a very bold statement that you have gotten on the side of satan.' Yes, and I believe it, trust and believe, I believe it because if you are not for me, then you are against me. There is no gray, there is no lukewarm. There is a line, you are either on my side or you are not. You do not play volley ball on top of the net, you play it on one side or the other, the opponents are very clear. So I want us to be clear about the fact that we are designed to help another individual, we are designed to help all people who belongs to us.

Now we want to get into semantics, but technically, if they are in your general vicinity, they belong to you. If there is any type of relationship being built for whatever the reason, they belong to you. At the end of everyday ask yourself, who belongs to me and why do they belong to me, because at the end of the day, they belong to you. So no matter how you want to get around it, these are the people that are in your midst, in your area, within your reach and designed for you to be responsible for. If you cannot figure out that you are responsible for them, then you will be shown.

You see, God spoke directly to Cain, God spoke directly to Cain and told him, this is your brother and you saw him last, that was on you. Genesis 4:10-15 reads, ¹⁰ The LORD said, "What have you done? Listen! Your brother's blood cries out to Me from the ground. ¹¹ Now you are under a curse and driven from the ground, which opened its mouth to receive your brother's blood from your hand. ¹² When you work the ground, it will no longer yield its crops for you. You will be a restless wanderer on the earth." ¹³ Cain said to the LORD, "My punishment is more than I can bear.¹⁴ Today You are driving me from the land, and I will be hidden from Your presence; I will be a restless wanderer on the earth, and whoever finds me will kill me." ¹⁵ But the LORD said to him, "Not so; anyone who kills Cain will suffer vengeance seven times over." Then the LORD put a mark on Cain so that no one who found him would kill him.

Did Cain not consider the consequences of his actions, his behavior. Likewise, we should consider our actions, so you reap and so shall you sow. Align ourselves with the word of God so we can help who belongs to us, what we can do to help others in their time of need because we would have a time of need. Everyone does, in our lives, everyone needs each other. We have to get to that position where we get past this whole point of selfishness and step out and help each other. As I mentioned, I had no true incentive in helping my nephew, however, I am going to help my nephew because I feel that helping him is what I am supposed to do. This is my job as his aunt, and as an older, wiser person and as an individual who has influence and used that very influence to help a young man. He is going to be accountable for everything else, but I did my part.

So from time to time, you can ask yourself am I doing everything I can to help the people around me, or am I focused on self with the mirror and everything is all about me? That is no way to really live. We need to get past that and get to a point where we can say to ourselves we are doing what we are supposed to do for one another and therefore, we can be accountable to God in a better fashion.

We are going to be accountable for the health and wellbeing of one another. Jesus commands us to love and serve one another. We are not able to function fully in our role for several reasons. Number one, again, the issue of Cain is very clear, he was jealous of what the Lord gave Abel. Let us look at our situation. We have been jealous of someone who has something that we wanted but we do not know what it took to get that. We do not understand the suffering. We do not understand their sacrifices. We do not understand any of that even if they belonged to us, and we are not self-assigned. That accountability is handed to us through God. By virtue of that accountability, we are on an assignment. Elizabeth was assigned to Mary. Eli was assigned to the widow woman. The twelve disciples were assigned to Jesus. Ananias was assigned to Saul. Paul was assigned to Timothy. We all have an assignment. Nathan was assigned to David. I am assigned to some persons, and it is my responsibility that those persons get the things that they need based on what I have to give them and I have been given those things to give to them by God. I did not create them myself, I did not make those relationships happen myself. Those were orchestrated and ordained by God for me to give away to somebody else. I tell people all of the time, I am not relegated to sharing what I think is enough. I can give all of my knowledge away. Why? Because I am not going to lose anything in the process; I am not going to lose a thing. It is all up to the individuals whether they use it or not, or they use it in the time that they were designed to use it. But that is not my job to stand in another person's way of not making any progress as a result of my lack of giving what I was designed to give them what it is I have, freely and willingly, with a great attitude and a very fabulous disposition. What does all this means to us, those fancy words, stop thinking more of yourself that you ought, whatever you know you learned from somewhere or somebody, give it away to somebody else so we can keep this going. It is a cyclical activity that has to happen, and this is what we are responsible for.

'Why is it my day to watch them? I just get tired of telling them and repeating myself over and over again.' I understand that, I feel you, I totally understand. But I guarantee you this, when I put it on my mind that was tired of repeating things to people, and telling people things that they do not respond to, immediately, proactively, right when I designed it, the Holy Spirit tapped me on my shoulder and said, 'Ma'am, I told you something this morning that you still haven't done. I told you five things yesterday that you still haven't done. And ten the day before that. And twenty the day before that and forty the day before that.'

Pretty soon, the Holy Spirit shared with me that even I do not follow His design and His rules and I am not completely obedient at all times, so dare I not judge another for them not taking what I said, which I think is fabulous and so true and so productive and make them respond in my time when I do not respond in God's time. Dare I not judge them. So I give them what I am supposed to give them and I leave it there. Wisdom will set in at one point and the Holy Spirit will bring it to their remembrance as He does for each of us to say this is the time you use that information that Onedia gave you like three years ago, and then all of a sudden, here we are using the information we already had possession of.

As a leader of a major retail brand, I coach and cross train everyone for the entire business. I let everybody know what they needed to know. One young man did not see the value of what it is that I did and he took it for granted. He thought it standard. He thought it was par. He did not appreciate it. When he asked me one day to transfer him to another store, I shared the process. He transferred to another location. One day at the new location, he worked an eight hour shift in the fitting room and was bored. One day somebody asked him did he know how to do some other things. He was used to doing so many things so said, 'Absolutely,' and then he ran down the list of things he knew under my training, which is when he realized that everybody was not like me and what he had taken for granted has become a very useful asset for him in his life. He thanked me and apologized, but he had to see it somewhere else.

Sometimes, that is how we are, we have to see it somewhere else, the very thing that someone says to you today means nothing; you do not have a sense of urgency attached. Maybe it was the tone or how it was delivered but when someone else presents it a little bit differently, can give you a little better example, can show you a little bit of difference, then all of a sudden we understand because the delivery was different, the presentation was different, your mind frame was different, your heart was in a different place, and you now search for knowledge that you previously have not even considered before. Now, you are in a different place, and now you can make it happen. So all of that said, what we need to understand and ask ourselves is 'are we in a position to receive what God has for us and who He is sending it through?' Sometimes, the vehicle by which we get things is not dressed up like we thought or not being like we thought or whatever it is that we think, but at the same time, we have to be in a position to say, this is what we want to be able to find out. It is my day to watch them.

I heard this phrase from someone because I asked her where someone was and she said, 'I do not know. It is not my day to watch them.' I thought it was so cute because what she was simply saying was that she was minding her own business and those people were not her responsibility. However, about three hours later, her phone rang because one of her kids got locked out of the house and she had to go home to let her child into the house. It was her day to watch them. She walked out of that building and never looked back, she was not worried about her job or her position or what was said or anything, because her kids were her responsibility, there were her number one priority.

And so at the end of every day, we have to ask ourselves who belongs to us? How are we treating those who belong to us? What is it that we needed to give to them so that they can have what they need to be successful so that they represent us well when they know that they belong to us?

My nephew has my last name. So anytime someone sees him, that knows me, even if they do not know that he is my nephew, because of his last name, they will ask him, do you know, Onedia Gage? And he is going to say, 'yes, she is my aunt.' In the meantime, while he is doing whatever he is doing, his behavior, his actions also represent me because I belong to him, too. And so in that mutual belonging, there has to be a format where we tell each other you belong to me— you have got my name on you. This means do not embarrass me and I won't embarrass you. You see, that is all God wants us to understand, wherever you are, whatever you are doing, whatever is going on in your life, your name has God attached to it. I wear God's name on me, so the things that I do not do, things that I do do, things which get me in trouble, there is a point where God is taking the risk. God is taking the risk for what it is that I am doing or not doing, the information that I have or do not have, and if I stop another person from getting to where they need to be with God because I have not given them information and I won't give into them, then I am wrong.

They are wrong because they need information to make it. I am wrong because I am withholding very valuable information from them. We have to ask ourselves what a life would it be if Elizabeth did not talk to Mary and Mary did not have

Elizabeth? If John the Baptist was not accountable and did not belong to Jesus, when he introduced the way? What if there was no Ananias and he said to Jesus, 'no matter what, I am not talking to Saul because he is a murderer,' and he disregarded that conversation that Jesus had with him and shared with him in Acts 9? What if Jesus said, 'I am the keep to this information to Myself and I am not going to share anything with you all, My Father's work will all be completed and I have decided that I will not share anything with you all because I am bitter because I have to die for you all, some of you do not even love Me, but I am dying for the very ones of who do not love me as well as the very ones who do?' What if it were like that? What if Nathan had said, 'God I will not deliver that message to David. David is king. You made him King; he is ruler over me too.' What if David had not received it the way he did?

We have to go into that relationship with a humble spirit. Just because you belong to me does not mean I lord over you, it means that I am going to be responsible for you and sharing with you all things I need to share with you. So understand that the people around us belong to us, we need to act like it. We are made to help each other. Stop being selfish. And we are held accountable for the health and the well-being of one another as Jesus commanded us so respond in kind. It is very critical that we understand this because it goes far into generations. It goes into everything that we have done. It goes further into our lives. David had sinned. Nathan came to rebuke him and hold him accountable. David immediately repented. The punishment took place and David went on to have Bathsheba conceive a great man: King Solomon.

Am I my brother's keeper? What a haughty question to ask God. Why is it my responsibility? Because He made it your job, like He made you somebody's job. We want to thank the Lord for who we belong to, the one who takes care of us, who sees after us, who helps us get to the next level, who helps us get to the point where need to be as well, we want to give over to them—our thanks.

So Lord God, how we bless and thank You for this day for this word. We thank You for this message. We thank You for all the charge and challenge that each and every one to go forward and act like the person You have designed for us and taking responsibility for them and ourselves and doing exactly what it is you called us forward to do. Lord God, we thank You for understanding what it is You want from us as a sinner, what it is You need from us and to understand how to minister to them all. In Jesus' name, we have prayed for these blessings. Amen.

With His Hands
John 20:24-31

Jesus Appears to Thomas

[24] Now Thomas (also known as Didymus), one of the Twelve, was not with the disciples when Jesus came. [25] So the other disciples told him, "We have seen the Lord!"

But he said to them, "Unless I see the nail marks in His hands and put my finger where the nails were, and put my hand into His side, I will not believe."

[26] A week later His disciples were in the house again, and Thomas was with them. Though the doors were locked, Jesus came and stood among them and said, "Peace be with you!" [27] Then He said to Thomas, "Put your finger here; see my hands. Reach out your hand and put it into my side. Stop doubting and believe."

[28] Thomas said to Him, "My Lord and my God!"

[29] Then Jesus told him, "Because you have seen Me, you have believed; blessed are those who have not seen and yet have believed."

The Purpose of John's Gospel

[30] Jesus performed many other signs in the presence of His disciples, which are not recorded in this book. [31] But these are written that you may believe that Jesus is the Messiah, the Son of God, and that by believing you may have life in His name.

Oh Lord God, how we thank You for this day, this time, with its beauty and all the things that are related to what it is You have us to do today. Lord God, we thank You for Your purpose in our lives. We thank You for Your gifts You give and how You share excellence with us. So Lord God today as we walk around in Your word, let us not take anything for granted. Let us not misuse and mistake anything for the messages that You have for each of us today. Afresh and anew. So Lord, I thank You right now for forgiving us of our sin. I thank You for allowing us to forgive those who trespass against us with an open heart, an open mind, and an open spirit forgiving as You would. Lord, I thank You right now for being able to allow us to do just what You do. It is in Your Son Jesus' name we pray and ask these blessings. Amen.

With His Hands

First of all, I want to define His. His could mean anybody. The hands of Jesus. The hands of God through Jesus. It is going to be a bit complex to just talk about Jesus' hands without talking about God's hands, but we are going to try the best that we can. With His hands, Jesus did some powerful things. I believe that we can agree on that without exception. We also want to consider that fact that with His hands He did some profound things. We want to talk about them and how that translates to us.

The Challenge

Now, I like Thomas. I like Thomas because Thomas speaks the truth. Thomas does not allow you to just walk up to him and just say anything. He wants proof. Now, Thomas let it be known that the disciples really had no influence over his life. He let it be known that they were not influential because of their wayward faith. He then helped them understand, "There is no way for me to just believe you. Above all else to believe you? I am not believing you." Now you have to ask yourself, why would Thomas do that based on things that have previously happened? We have to consider the fact that Thomas has seen the disciples' behavior, has seen the disciples in action, and he has been walking with them for some period of time now. Thomas has reasons not to trust the other disciples, or at least be skeptical.

The whole goal was to figure out how to translate their faith and share with others. Because the disciples by now have been through some things. They have seen some stuff. They have seen enough things so their belief should not be that fragile and that is the point that Jesus is making. "Isn't there are enough things they have been through? There is enough evidence you have seen. There are enough miraculous activities that you witnessed that you should not have a weak faith. Your belief should not be based on what you can see and what you can experience personally."

Sometimes you have to take somebody else's word for information. Thomas was just not ready take their word for it. He did not believe them on that level. Now we might have people that no matter what it is, we do not believe anything that comes out of their mouth. Thomas was one of the 12, which meant there were 10 people telling him this. And of course his concern and my concern would have been 'how is it that I have missed this event.'

'How is this possible? Where was I? What was I doing that required me to be away from the position where I could see Jesus for myself? You saw Him. Why was it that I wasn't able to see Him for myself? What was I doing? Was I at the grocery? Was I at the mall when God came and showed Himself to you all?

Why did not anyone call for me? When He unveiled Himself to you all, what was I doing?'

Well, of course my concern is the same: 'Now, I have got to believe you guys? You all saw Him alive? Hmmm....' I am thinking I better proceed cautiously about that situation. I understand Thomas; I get it. This is an important occurrence. This is another once-in-a-lifetime event. Thomas needs processing time to consider the implications of this unwitnessed event. Thomas is dealing with himself about his whereabouts and activities.

It is important to understand who you believe when you are presented with information, especially life changing, unbelievable information. This is who you are trusting for information. So we do not even want to go through the litany of the disciples and their activities and behavior. They have done things, which offers you understandable levels of concern, and could easily become consumed with it. I cannot believe you do not believe why we having such issues. So obviously, Peter comes to mind.

THE REVEAL

In verse 27, Then He said to Thomas, "Put your finger here; see My hands." When Jesus gives Thomas His hand, it made me think of the things that Jesus had done with that hand. So let's walk through those scriptures and let's walk through those occurrences, so we can understand what he has done with those hands.

HIS HAND OF AUTHORITY

His hand of authority. There are several things He does in a very authoritative manner—because of His hands, with His hands. One of these events is the Lord's Supper. When He introduces the blood of the covenant and the bread of the covenant, He would not eat or drink from those elements until He joined with us again. When He offers His father's house, which has many mansions is an exercise of His hand of authority.

We have seen that hand before: when God offered it to Moses. He says extend your staff across this Red Sea and I will part it for you. That hand of authority is not given out lightly. It is not given out without the power that it is designed to possess. It produces the result it is designed to produce. That hand of authority needs to be carefully considered. Because of Him, the authority is just that. That hand of authority is not to be questioned and not to be denied.

His Hand of Love

Then there is the hand of love. John 17. He spends time sharing with us. John 15:13: ¹³ Greater love has no one than this: to lay down one's life for one's friends. He is the hand of love. He is a very exhibit of what love is and what love was defined to be. Because of God's great love for us, He sent Jesus. His hand of love extends out to us. His hand of love is still extended to Peter when He said come and Peter got up and Jesus immediately reached for him. That is the hand of love. When He took the little children in Matthew into Himself, that was His hand of love. The Lord expects us to use that same hand of love when we are dealing with one another. He said love one another as you love thyself. He meant that; a problem we have is that we do not use our own hands to love ourselves. That is how we start our own problems.

His Hand of Compassion

Then there is the hand of compassion. John 11:35 says, 'Jesus wept'; that is compassion. When the lady touched the hem of His garment in Luke, He said,

'He felt power go away from Him.' He said, 'Your faith has made you whole daughter.' That is the hand of compassion.

HIS HAND OF POWER

The hand of power. We talk about His mighty hand of power. And when He uses that power to fulfill the word of God. I am most moved and most stifled by His hands power when He puts His hands together and prayed. Those are the most powerful positions for His hands to be in. That would be John 17 and Matthew 6, when He teaches us how to pray.

HIS HAND OF RESURRECTION

And then there is the hand of resurrection. His touch and His calling of Lazarus out of the tomb, for the daughter who's presumed dead and He said, 'She was sleeping.' The hand of resurrection.

HIS HAND OF HEALING

There is His hand of healing. The fact that He has just made people whole. Jesus struck Saul blind and brought him to the place that He wanted him to settle down, reflect and meditate so He could hear from Jesus. And then He sent in Ananias and he was healed. Or the girl who was demon possessed. Or the man by the pool with his mat. 'Do you want to walk?' His hand of healing.

HIS HAND OF LIFE

And then there is His hand of the life. When you look at His actual hands that were nailed just for me, those nails did not harm His hands to the point of non-use. Not only were they useable but they were more powerful now then they have ever been. The hands of Life. And when He holds that life, when He holds our lives in His hands, He holds them delicately and gently but with strength and power, not so as to crush but so as to nurture. And to discipline and to love: All at the same time.

HIS HAND OF RELATIONSHIPS

And then there's the hand of relationships. Jesus had a knack for hanging out in interesting places. None of us accepted our salvation in His name until He came and all had to be shown and shared Him upon His arrival. Even those that follow Him based on what He did, what He said, and what they saw, still had to accept Him and His offering of salvation. But He only really hung out until that relationship was forged. Understand that that hand of relationship was very important because He wants a relationship with those He is called: all of us. And He has to spend time with us in that relationship. And once He puts His hand on that relationship, that relationship is going to be different. So likewise, as you consider our relationship with Christ and how we forge that relationship and where He has His hands on us, we have to give some consideration to what that is and what that means and how that is made complete. Jesus was challenged by His relationship with sinners, the woman at the well, and the Samaritan woman. People questioned His Christianity because He hung out with and sought sinners. However, He says to us, 'Who can share Christ if we do not spend time with them. How can we do that? How is it possible that we can move people from yet sinners to being able to go forward if we do not have our hands on that relationship?' We have to put our hands on our relationships. We do not win others to Christ other than handling that relationship. That relationship becomes critical. It becomes important. That hand of relationship is very important.

HIS HAND OF REDEMPTION

The hand of redemption. There is a woman scheduled to be stoned. There is a woman they are about to be stoned and He walks up. He draws a line in the sand and He says, 'let he who is without sin cast the first stone.' And without any further ado or conversation, the crowd is gone. Without any further ado or conversation, the crowd is gone. He forgives her for her sin and tells her to go and sin no more. That is the life we're working for: The hand of redemption. We want to be in a process or in a position where we want to be in His redemptive measures; be where He redeems, be where He saves, be where He makes whole. That is our goal is to be whole. Be made whole. As we move forward, we need to consider how we get into the measure of redemption. His hand of redemption: How do we get there?

HIS HAND OF FORGIVENESS

Likewise, His hand of forgiveness. One of the disciples asks, 'How many times should I forgive? Jesus responds, '70 times 7.' The disciple questions, '7 times 7?' 'No, 70 times 7.' He implied that forgiveness would be infinite. Forgiveness should be continuous. And it should be done lovingly.

HIS HAND OF DISCIPLINE

His hand of discipline. They were selling wares in His Father's house, in the synagogue. He takes and turns the table over and says, 'you have made My Father's house a den of robbers.' That behavior is in and of itself discipline. ''Peter, this is not the time for that. He takes the servant's ear and puts it back on his head and then His hands of healing and His hand of discipline showed up at the same time.

His Hand of Wisdom

And then there is His hand of wisdom. His hand of wisdom distinctively shares with us those things which we do not have vision of. The Alabaster jar holds expensive perfume. Wisdom is using the perfume that has been released from the alabaster jar to put upon Him. He says, 'I will not be with you always but your poor will be with you always. What she is doing is timely because she knows that she will not see me in this capacity again. So, do not use the poor as a reason to miss a life-changing activity.' Sometimes when we are not wise enough to recognize how our situation is a gift and this will never happen again.

Solomon spends a lot of time sharing proverbial lessons for us that we often do not seek, and we often do not heed, but we have to seek those nuggets. Also, we have to seek that time when His hand of wisdom is upon us in our daily lives but we ignore or we do not consider; we do not seek and so we have got to be more in tune with His hand so we can get the wisdom that we need so that we will be equipped to carry out His will. Part of our wisdom is to know when to do what and there are often times when we have made poor decisions and poor choices based on that fact that we are not paying attention in a wise manner. Or not paying attention with wisdom on our mind or with our intention.

His Hand of Knowledge

The hand of knowledge. He says for you do not know why I am here and I am going to do exactly what I came to do and that is to preach the gospel. Forgive them for they do not know what they do Father. In those two places, He shares with us His knowledge that is far beyond our very comprehension. And we should heed to that and use that as an example.

HIS HANDS OF PROVISION

He washed the disciple's feet in order to teach us to serve others. He teaches with those hands. He serves others with those hands. And His feeding with those hands. He has provided a lot with those hands. He more than adequately provided for us.

WITH HIS HANDS

With His hands, He has served God just like He was designed. We seek to do the same. Jesus has hands which we just are appreciative of access to. He guides us and keeps us.

Amen.

Lord God, how we bless You and thank You for Your hands. And for what those hands have done and delivered. For what those hands have redeemed. For those problems that those hands have solved. Lord God, we thank You right now for the fact that Your hands have saved us it heals us. It undergirds us. It strengthens us. It provides for power and it provides us with peace. Lord God, afresh we thank You for forgiving us of our sins. We thank You for Your compassion in our lives. We thank You for the love that You give. Unashamedly, without limits. We thank You, Lord God, right now in Your Son's Jesus' name, we pray. We thank You for this time today. Amen.

Some Unresponsive Clay
Isaiah 29:16; 45:9, 64:8

¹⁶ You turn things upside down,
  as if the potter were thought to be like the clay!
Shall what is formed say to the one who formed it,
  "You did not make me"?
Can the pot say to the potter,
  "You know nothing"?

Isaiah 29:16 (NIV)

⁹ "Woe to those who quarrel with their Maker,
  those who are nothing but potsherds
  among the potsherds on the ground.
Does the clay say to the potter,
  'What are you making?'
Does your work say,
  'The potter has no hands'?

Isaiah 45:9 (NIV)

⁸ Yet you, LORD, are our Father.
  We are the clay, you are the potter;
  we are all the work of your hand.

Isaiah 64:8 (NIV)

Father God, how we love You and bless Your holy name, we thank You right now Lord God for what it is You have for each of us and thank You right now for using me as a vessel to do Your work, Your will. But I want You to have Your way today Lord, and I thank You right now that You are our focus, the keeper of our heads, perfecter of our faith. Lord, right now I just thank You for what You're doing, what You're going to do, what You have already done, and so that we are able to give You glory and honor. We thank You for forgiving us of our sins. We thank You for using us according to Your purpose and we thank You Lord God, for being able to give You some of what You deserve. Lord, we ask to improve it on a daily basis and we thank You for this message today that we understand what our role is, what our job is, and what it is that you want us to do, be able to do as Your children. Lord God, I thank You right now for what You have said today. We thank You for covering us completely. Under Your anointing, and it is in Your Son, Jesus name that I pray and ask You to bless us. Amen.

In my research, I spent time understanding the properties and details of clay. For the purpose of our conversation today, I really wanted to understand what clay was, and what was it used for and why it is used in that manner.

Clay comes from many geographical areas. So the clay in South American, the clay in Canada, and the clay in Martha's Vineyards and the clay in California are all going to be different. And because they are all going to be different, they're going to have different properties. They're going to have different things that make their minerals denser or looser, more flexible, lack in flexibility, lack in plasticity; all of which factors into the shaping of the clay into pottery. All clay is different.

It is similar our dialect. You can listen to someone and say, "They're from the South," "They're from North," "They're from Canada," "They're from New England," "They're from Africa", and "They're from Australia." There's a tone in your voice, there's an inflection of your voice that allows for us to understand what your speech origin is.

Likewise, clay has some of those same distinguishing characteristics. The clay is designed to be transformed into pottery. For that to happen, there are some elements required. There is a wheel. There is the potter, the creator of this pottery, the molder, the artistic creator in this whole relationship. You put some clay on the wheel, formless and lifeless, and the potter's job is to take what it is given, the clay, and in its foremost capacity and raggedy as it is, and unattractive as it appears, to take it and mold it into something that is very beautiful, extremely gorgeous, something that is coveted, something that could be expensive, and something that contributes.

You take the clay, then you get a certain amount of it. You take the clay, you add water and other chemicals to it to add that plasticity. And then once you do that, that flexibility gives you the opportunity to form the shape that you desire.

This clay is not something that all of us are aware of how to find, acquire, mix and or preserve in a fashion that it is designed to be done. However, the potters are those skilled individuals. The potters are going to be able to do just what we are talking about. The potters are going to have skills in that area. Now, one of the tools that the potters use in addition to the clay are water and other chemicals, they also use a pottery wheel. We are not pottery experts.

On this pottery wheel, the clay is turning. It is turning at a certain rate of speed, and it is turning in a certain direction. It does that all the time, it doesn't slow or quicken without cause. The potter is holding the reigns on the quickness and the slowness of this wheel. As the potter has the wheel turning, he's using that wheel to shape the pottery. And while he's shaping the pottery, he's creating that piece he will later be proud of. There is some craftiness involved, there is some creativity involved and during this period of time, realize that the potter is thinking. The potter has a plan, the potter has a considerable effort that he's put in or she's put in to designing what they want this vase to look like, this consumable product to look like.

Let's trust and believe, when they sat down at the potter's wheel, where they gather the clay, when they mix the water and the chemicals together, and when they made the appointment for the piece of clay that is now shaped into a form and submitted as an appointment to go to the kiln, they had a design in mind. The potter did not just sit down at the table and on a chair for hours shaping and forming without having an idea in his mind or her mind on what this was going to look like at the final table. He did not sit down to make a vase but made an ashtray instead or by accident. No, he did not sit down to make the tall vase and but only had enough clay for a bud vase. He did not sit down to make you know a floor urn and get just a bowl, he did not do that. When he sat down to make the large three foot vase that you put in the corner and that you put the tall trees in, when he sat down that is what he wanted to do. It was intentional.

The potter doesn't make any accidents. The potter goes in knowing that he is designing just what he wants to sell. What he can be proud of. When the potter walks into a room and recognizes his pieces, he gets a little proud. You would too, if you had created something. It is like as a parent, you walk into class and know your child has done those pieces, that is my child's work, that is my child. You already know this, you get excited because you were part of the creation of that human being. You were used as a vessel to create a human being. Same thing when you use a vase for flowers - now what's prettier, the vase or the flowers? They really come together for a whole package.

So understand, God created us from the depths of the ground and as the Potter gathers His clay, so You shaped me. As clay on a potter's wheel, You shaped me and my personality, my will and my way. There are times when I know that God has wanted me to think about it differently. He wanted to think about things differently. He made Onedia Gage and there are times where He wants to say: "Ma'am, look here. That is not what I said for you to do." And likewise, the potter has some of those same concerns at times.

I am His creation, without any input from me. I just mentioned a moment ago, that the God we serve formed us from the ground, out of dust. When He made Adam, He took a scoop of dirt. He shaped and formed and molded him. And when He shaped and formed and molded him. He molded him into a human being. He made his arms, and He made his fingers, and He made his nails, and He made his cuticles, He made his eyes, his eyebrows, his eyelashes. He even made those lines between our eyebrows which we push together to show our frustration, disgust, anger and anguish; He made that too. He made all the things about us and when He formed Adam up and He blew His breath 'puffs' on him, He blew into him – life.

Out the dust we were formed and then we became out of our mothers' wombs we were formed. And after all of that formation, I never was asked: "Do you want long hair or short hair? Do you want it a brown-black? Do you want it grey? Do you want speckles of grey at a certain age? Do you want all black hair the whole time? Do you want to be tall or short? Do you want to have long arms or short arms? Do you want to have small knees or medium size knees? What do you want for ears?" He never asked me a single thing. I did not make myself, I did not get to vote.

We need to ask ourselves 'are we doing what He created us to do, how are we handling what He created, how are we managing what He created?' If we can explain that, then we can go forward with what we are supposedly doing with what He created. Are we serving our purpose under His creation? I go on and say to understand that I did not get to pick, neither did you. Because of that, there are some things who need to manage as if it is the gift as it is because that is what it is: a gift.

I often view creation with a total stamp of a me that He may not totally approve of. Let me say it again – I often view creation with a total stamp of a me that He may not totally approve of. God created me. He did not ask me what I wanted to look like, be like, talk like, act like, walk like, love like, see like, think like, feel like, or be spirited like. He did not do any of that. What He did was He took me, understanding all of what He had planned in advance for me to do and He shaped me based on that work, which I am to do. It took me to understand that here's what I am, this is what God made. And He did not ask me, He does not need my help. Likewise, when I go to changing His creation, I'm out of order, I'm out of line.

You cannot go around changing the work of an author. When you copy someone's work and you do not give them credit, it is called plagiarism. Likewise, you cannot take their works and start rearranging it, it is in violation of the ethics code of scholastics, of academia. Who are you to tell the Potter that He doesn't know anything? He should have made my hair curly without need of a product called 'wet', or a product called 'Pink Lotion' or a product called 'Mixed Chicks', He should have made my hair without the need of all of that. He should have made my hair where it does this.

Who are you? Who gave you the authority to tell God what He should have done? After you started telling God, how likely it would have been better if you had done this. Excuse me!? In your finite wisdom, I guess we could say that, but guess what? You did not create yourself, you cannot recreate yourself and I need you to get back in line with His original creation. See I alter His creation without His consent. And just by virtue of the fact that He created me, He knows His will for my life. He knew me before He formed me. He already had this all blueprinted out and drawn up for me before I got here. How dare I say I am the bomb enough to tell Him: "You know what, You made a mistake, and You really should have done this instead with me." Who does that? Oh sorry, we do, every day. So, when we decided to alter His creation, you think the clay can change his color? You think the clay can just change his design? I do not want to be a fat squatty vase, but I want to be a thin slender tall vase. You think the clay can change itself? Absolutely not. How do you think God feels when we change and we modify and we manage and we mess with His creation? How do you think He feels? What do you think He thinks of us when we do that?

I am resisting Him in my mind, body and soul, yet still call Him – Father. I am resisting Him in my mind, body and soul, yet still call Him – Daddy. You see, as a child I was very inquisitive, precocious, daredevil, no fear, and no boundaries. I would just get in there and take care of it and go for what I knew. And I was without fear, without that kind of reservation. I did not even think it was a problem. But because of some of that activity, I was disobedient to my parents. And yet while I was disobedient, I still called her mother and I still called him daddy. I still expected them to provide, protect, preserve, and make it happen for me. When I asked you for something, I expected it to arrive within the hour. I expected it to arrive within the next few days. I expected you to solution, solve, remedy, fix, nurture, cover, love, handle, will, feed, clothe, shelter and I expected you to do all those things regardless of what I had just done. Broke your dish, talked back, stayed on the phone longer than what I was supposed to, did not do all of my homework and got a B instead of an A. That is what I'm talking about.

We do these things to God and guess what we do, we tell Him 'I'm going to disobey You willfully, and I'm going to expect for You to cover me just as You did when I wasn't disobedient.' I expect You to keep me in your loving arms unconditionally, even though I am willfully and purposely being disobedient. Are we sure that the path that we want to take as clay?

You see, our words say that we are telling God that we know more than Him when we determine that we are going to do exactly what He said to not to do.

So, verse 16 says: 'You turn things upside down, as if the potter were thought to be like the clay! Shall what is formed say to the one who formed it, "You did not make me, you know nothing."? Can the pot say to the potter?

Do not think so, do not think so. When we look at our behavior, our willful disobedience, the fact that we want to tell Him how to make us, and how to mold and how to shape us and how to do what it is He's already called us and forward put faith in us to do. Yet if we doubt, if we have fear, then we are without faith.

Clay turns into pottery. And the pottery is sold or traded for goods and services, money if you will. You see, pottery is a vase or a paperweight or it is an ashtray. Pottery can be turned into a bowl or a pot. And let's be clear, that piece of clay; that pottery is going to serve its purpose. That pottery is going to hold those green beans and those collard greens, that pottery is going to hold that macaroni and cheese. It is going to hold those flowers for Mother's Day, Birthday, Anniversary, Wedding, Thanksgiving, Christmas, Easter, Mother's Day, Father's Day and New Year's. It is going to hold the coins, because the vase can be used for the flowers or the bank. But it is going to serve its purpose. You see, what happens when a piece of pottery breaks and is no longer useful, we discard that piece of pottery. You do not keep that chipped vase. Why? Because it is no longer useful. Matter of fact it becomes downright dangerous because if that baby gets a hold of it, then she could cut herself. If something happens to your baby, then you know how you're going to respond.

So likewise, we need to understand that we are resisting Him with all of who we are. Yet we call Him Father and we expect the Lord to come to our aid, to come to our assistance, to love us unconditionally, to forgive us of our sins. All of those that were definitely premeditated. And then above all else, above all else, above all else, some days we walk out of our home and do not even thank Him for the life He's breathed into us so that we have the functionality to resist our Creator. Yes, I'm going to say it again, we have the nerve, the audacity, the unmitigated gall to not even thank Him for what it is He's done for us already and we are going to start with and we should have started with the functionality of our lungs because without the functionality or without that breath rolling through our lungs we would not even have the ability to get up and disobey.

Could He treat us like the potter, the pottery that is not functional? Oh absolutely. Yes, He could. He could just starve us. He could cancel our assignment. He could end our purpose right here on earth. Because guess what, He is not running out of clay soon. He is the Creator. He can get Him some more clay from anywhere.

Well let's talk about what is 'Unresponsive Clay'. Clay that does not do what a potter wants it to do. There's a specific amount of clay and a specific amount of water and other chemicals that are used to put together this pottery. When you take that clay and you mix it with that water and you mold it, but if it doesn't respond properly, if it is hard and it doesn't want to be flexible and plastic-like and if it doesn't want to be moved and shaped, the potter then decides what is going to happen with this unresponsive clay. The potter may move to the side and say: "Well I'll see about it later" or the potter may just discard it on the spot and say: "I have another whole batch of clay, I can just pull me some more out." The potter does not give the clay a second chance. But our God, the God who chose us, the God who is our Potter, gives us countless chances. Chances we do not even consider a second chance but He gave it to us anyway.

So here we are, what happens to 'Unresponsive Clay'? Now, we want to know why is the clay unresponsive. Well maybe that clay was a bad batch. Those minerals respond differently from Amazon, versus Canada, versus Hawaii, versus Australia, versus Europe. That response is different. We need to understand our response is as well different. And what we want to realize is that it doesn't have to be different, it is not supposed to be different, it shouldn't necessarily neither be based on those differences, the clay should just simply respond. If it is six scoops of clay and twelve drops of water, then that should be the formula. But not so much. Sometimes it is six scoops of clay and fifteen drops of water, sometimes it is six scoops of clay and six drops of water but whatever it is, what needs to happen is that we need to be consumed and concerned with how do we become 'Responsive Clay.'

When we are unresponsive, how do we know? Well, I'm glad you asked. Our responsiveness is based on God's word. You see, there's been one above of all of His creation. We are up to billions of people and there's been One who's been responsive. You see, His assignment was to come and save us. Our sorry unresponsive selves from our premeditated and not being able to turn away from our sin. He was real responsive. Because when you say love, He loved; when you say save, He saves; when you say heal, He heals; and when you say cry, He cries and He is compassionate. He is the definition of all of those things.

We put some attachments and some restrictions and some conditions on our love and compassion, on our service and our healing. That is 'Unresponsive Clay'. When you just do not want to hug and check on and see about and when you just do not want to allow the other person the benefit of the doubt. Give him the second chance, give him that moment to come back but instead we say: "Sorry, but no, no, you cannot talk to me now, that is over with. I gave you all I'm supposed to give you." But what if God did us like that as His creation? Oh no, we cannot tolerate that, 'Lord, give me one more chance, Lord, give me one more chance'. Now, do not get that confused with that rhythm and blues song. No, do not get that confused. So when we say: "Lord, forgive us of our sins." It is something we do not count them anymore, we just say "Lord, forgive us of our sins," and we hope that covers everything. But we are supposed to say: "Lord, forgive me for putting her off on the freeway and calling her names other than a child of God. Lord, forgive me for not loving unconditionally. Forgive me for quitting on what You designed for me. Lord, thank You for making me who I am. But I do not like none of what You're talking about, I cannot do none of that." Unresponsive clay.

That is what we know. We do not need a reminder, we do not need anybody to tap us on the shoulder and tell us we are being unresponsive. We know that! Because we are intelligent and He made us that way. We are loving and we are giving it when we want to, how we want to and in increments where you have to earn it. If you take one step, I'm going to take one and if you take two steps, I'm going to take one and if you take three steps, I'm going to take a one and a half. We do not even explain that upfront. We just give people and spoon it to them and we hope it is okay, we expect it to be fine. When it is really not how we are loved at all.

But there was One who He said: "Go over there to those unresponsive pieces of clay and die for them so that I may save My own world that which I created and even those who have a hand in Your death, We'll save them too." And on the cross, with spear in His side and the crown of thorns on His head, He says: "Forgive them Father, for they know not what they do." Oh yes, He did. And we are not saying that. We are not saying: "Forgive us Father for we know our sins." We tell our Lord: "Why don't You want to do something to them, and why do they still get to have everything they have even though they have mistreated me?" That is what we say. Some unresponsive clay.

As we transition to figuring out how to be more responsive, how to be more like Christ who is the ultimate definition of 'responsive clay.' I want us to remember, and realize and recognize and be able to feel for and send for some responsiveness, consider what we are called to do. Our calling has nothing to do with being a Preacher, Teacher, none of that, not gifts – calling. Being in the likeness of His image, you have love without strings. The love when they do not love you back, to heal those that may not deserve it, to go places where we would not normally go, to do things we would not normally do. And what it is we are doing to the glory of God, not the mediocrity which we feel like we can get away with. Oh yeah, that is some responsive clay and that is the example we have in Christ Jesus who hung, bled and died and was resurrected for ours sins. So there we have it.

I pray to be more responsive, I pray to be more interactive in my responses. I pray that my behavior leads others to do the same.

Lord God, how we bless You and thank You each day for being merciful to one and each of us, Lord we thank You right now for the power within the words that You have sent us today: How to be more responsive to You, to others, how to be more responsive to You because of You, because You are God and God alone. Thank You right now for sending Jesus, the most responsive clay ever known. Thank You right now Lord God for what You do. And what You do without and what You do because, and because not. Lord God, I thank You, I bless You, I thank You for using me as Your vessel. I thank You for who will hear and what this will do for their lives. Lord God I thank You right now for what it has done in my life. It is in Your Son Jesus' name that I pray and ask You these blessings. Amen.

With a Dirty Heart and Some Horrible Motives
Romans 7:9-25

⁹ Once I was alive apart from the law; but when the commandment came, sin sprang to life and I died. ¹⁰ I found that the very commandment that was intended to bring life actually brought death.¹¹ For sin, seizing the opportunity afforded by the commandment, deceived me, and through the commandment put me to death. ¹² So then, the law is holy, and the commandment is holy, righteous and good.

¹³ Did that which is good, then, become death to me? By no means! Nevertheless, in order that sin might be recognized as sin, it used what is good to bring about my death, so that through the commandment sin might become utterly sinful.

¹⁴ We know that the law is spiritual; but I am unspiritual, sold as a slave to sin. ¹⁵ I do not understand what I do. For what I want to do I do not do, but what I hate I do. ¹⁶ And if I do what I do not want to do, I agree that the law is good. ¹⁷ As it is, it is no longer I myself who do it, but it is sin living in me. ¹⁸ For I know that good itself does not dwell in me, that is, in my sinful nature. For I have the desire to do what is good, but I cannot carry it out. ¹⁹ For I do not do the good I want to do, but the evil I do not want to do—this I keep on doing. ²⁰ Now if I do what I do not want to do, it is no longer I who do it, but it is sin living in me that does it.

²¹ So I find this law at work: Although I want to do good, evil is right there with me. ²² For in my inner being I delight in God's law; ²³ but I see another law at work in me, waging war against the law of my mind and making me a prisoner of the law of sin at work within me. ²⁴ What a wretched man I am! Who will

rescue me from this body that is subject to death? ²⁵ Thanks be to God, who delivers me through Jesus Christ our Lord!
So then, I myself in my mind am a slave to God's law, but in my sinful nature a slave to the law of sin.

Romans 7:9-25 (NIV)

WITH A DIRTY HEART AND HORRIBLE MOTIVES

The beginning of this topic is struggling with sin, and this is authored by Paul. Understand that Paul, again, is favored by Christ, is favored by God. So, for him to put out in writing that we are— that he is sinful and what happens to him is based on his sinful nature, is rather eye-opening. Paul is not favored because of sin, but because of his work, his admission of sin, and his repentance from sin. However, it is what we need to know and get a clear understanding of so that we ourselves can be equipped for what it is we are up against.

WE HAVE NO IDEA

What we do not know are several things. One, we do not understand our own behavior. Verse 15 reads, "I do not understand what I do." There's a point in our lives where we do not know what we do not know. When you do not know something, you do not know that you do not know it. And it sounds really strange, but until you're exposed to it, until it is shown to you, you do not know it. You just do not. It is not something you know.

One of the things that we do not know is we do not know ourselves that well. We do not know ourselves that well. We do not know who we are in its completeness and its totality. We do not know our full potential. We do not know who we are under certain circumstances, and in a certain situation. We can say beyond a shadow of a doubt, I will never be in this scenario, I will never do this. I'll never do that. However, when it comes to that situation, what will you do? You do not know that until you come upon that situation.

You thought you'd never pray out loud, yet you do. You thought you'd never do something, but yo''re doing that something. You thought you never could achieve that position, but yet you have done it. And so what we have to understand is that there is a potential for each of us to sin, and we need to recognize that potential exists: it is real. We need to orchestrate and behave in a manner that lets us know that. We need to behave that way. We need to behave in a fashion that reminds us that we have sinned, that we are able to sin. That we have the potential to sin, and that we have the ability to do so.

It is not something that is foreign or for someone else, it is not for someone else. It is for us; it is related to who we are and what we do. It is not about someone else. So you have got to ask yourself at whatever time, at whatever point, that we are people who have sin, and we are going to fall short of God's glory, so what are we going to do to manage that process? What are we going to do? We have got to ask ourselves that. We have got to understand.

And when we say we do not understand ourselves, 'I do not understand what I do,' we have got to also realize that you're not the only person who doesn't understand what you do. However, our Creator does understand what we do. I cannot say that He likes it, cannot say that He can find favor with it, and cannot say that He is going to excuse it. But He does know what we are going to do, and that is a very scary place for me, because I do not want to do those things; I do not want to be wrong in those areas. I do not want that.

I do not want to be in a position where God knows I'm going to sin. When I leave my home today, I do not want God to know that I'm going to sin when I leave. That is just so embarrassing. You're just going to sin today, that is just all there is to it, there's no way around it, it is going to happen. And to me, that is one of those things where I just say, 'oh my gosh, I just, I really wish that was not that case and situation.' I wish that were not the case and situation, but it is. Yet, it is. So, what we want to find ourselves doing and figuring out is making sure that we are then there to say, 'Lord God, we are trying to do better than what we think our best is.'

When he says, "For what I want to do I do not do, but what I hate I do," he has my attention: the sin is real. And we need to make sure that we understand why it is real. It is used to separate us from Christ. And as glued to Him as we think we are, there are methods by which the devil is going to use to get between the two of us.

When I named this sermon "With a Dirty Heart and Horrible Motives," it spoke to that level of sin. If we never do anything bad or wrong or sinful or spiteful; if we never do anything horrible, we just have to really examine our own heart and our own motives. For the most part, people are good. They have good intentions, they have good motives. But there's some days, each of us, at some point, has had a dirty heart and some less than honorable, or rather horrible, motives. And we need to be on watch for that because we need to put ourselves in a better position than that; so that we can avoid this sin.

What's going on with this dirty heart and horrible motives? So let's take revenge for instance. That is always a great topic. Someone's always after somebody because of something they've done to them. It is a retaliatory situation. Now let's talk about that. A horrible motive; to wish poorly on someone, to keep antagonizing someone just because you feel that you can and you can stir up a response out of them, just to pick at someone because you feel that they're the weaker vessel, and that you can take advantage of them, because of it. Those are horrible behaviors fueled by horrible motives.

I believe that every family should have a strong matriarch. I do not have one, but that doesn't mean that I'm going to bully anybody in the family for it, and I'm not going to be bullied by anybody as well. But what are your motives? What motives do you have when you are making your actions and when you're making decisions, what are you using for a motive? Are you being horrible to someone on purpose, and why is that? And why do you do that, and why do feel like it is okay to do that? Would you like to be treated that way? And the answer should be no. Then why would you do that someone else? Were you treated that way when you were in that same position? The answer is no. So why are you treating someone else that way?

We have got to be careful, extremely cautious, otherwise deliberately so, that we do not take advantage of another person or a situation. The fact of the matter is that that could come back: you'e going to reap what you sow.

That dirty heart is going to influence you to do things that are less than loving, less than being Christ-like, less than—it will put you in a position of being less than because you want to do something that is horrible. And when you do something basically horrible, you want to be sure that you know what the consequences are, and how far reaching they are and how long will they last.

We have to check ourselves; we are the only person who knows what's going on inside of our hearts, other than God, the Holy Spirit, and Christ. We have got to check those hearts, those heart details where we say, you know what, I need to get my heart right. I need to get my heart together. And I need to get my heart pointed back to God in such a fashion that I do not feel compelled to respond to everything that you do to me that should cause me to sin. I should be able to walk away.

The scripture says, "Create in me a clean heart, oh God," and that clean heart is going to contradict that dirty heart and horrible motives. I like how he confesses, "but it is sin that lives within me." He offers up the fact that the motives of his heart are not supposed to be ugly, yet they've turned into something terrible. That it is not supposed to be, but it is turned into that. And what we want to be able to do is avoid those two things with as much zeal as we possibly can.

WE NEED TO GET TO KNOW OURSELVES

As I told you, our first problem is that we do not know ourselves. The second thing is that we need to get to know ourselves. You see, we talked a moment ago about casting away that dirty heart and those horrible motives. You have got to ask yourselves, what makes this influence over me so strong? And do I need to ask for the escape that is established for me so that I can avoid the sin that is about to so easily encumber me? We have got to ask those questions because those are critical pieces to us. We have got to ask ourselves, how do I leave the horrible motives and the dirty heart? And be able to say with certainty this is who I am. This is where I reside; this is who you witness me to be.

I really find a problem with people who show one side of themselves to someone else, and they show a different side of themselves to another person. You know, they're really friendly outside the house: oh, she's so sweet. But she's mean as a beast at home. Meaner than the worst lion, meaner than a junkyard dog. That is a dirty heart. Why do you feel the need to fake it away from home? And the other question is, why isn't that the reverse? You should treat the people you live with and the people you claim to love, the people you share a last name with, better than you treat anybody else, but that is not the case.

So how do we ask for our life so we can get that back and where we can move around as God intended? How do we ask for that? How do we intend to ask for that? How do we ask the Lord to do that?

God Knows Us

Our third point is that God knows us. And what we need to do is get to know what He knows about us. Get to know the us that He created. And in some cases, that means resetting us back to the factory settings.

The one thing I hate about cell phone problems is the first thing that the customer service agent asks is to call back from a landline. 'We are going to reset your phone.' And I get immediately nervous, because I'm sitting here thinking there are 4000 contacts in my phone, there are 5,000 pictures in my phone, and there are documents and other important, non-retrievable items. And when she says to reset the phone, I just immediately cringe. But whatever the issue is that she's trying to solve requires us to go to the default settings and restore the factory settings. How were they created? And when in our mind's eye, we ask God to share with us how to fix the dirty heart and horrible motives, we have got to be willing to go back to the reset button, the default setting. Restore us at a different level. We need to get ready to do that.

Why do we need to do that? Well, in the technology world, we do not know where the virus or the problem started or took place; we do not know exactly what's responsible. And those people at the phone store, they're on a time limit. So the easiest, fastest, quickest thing to do is to just take it all off, just erase everything and start over. And then you can reload those things one at a time, and maybe during that reload, you'll find out what the problem is. Well, see, here's the problem— He could erase everything, and we should be able to go back to the factory settings, but we do not want to. And sometimes we want to keep a little dirt over here, and a little sin over there. We want to be able to reach back and get some of those components from time to time. I want us to be very cautious into how we move in that area. How do we move around in that area? Because it is very difficult to do. It is very difficult to live without our sins.

It is very difficult to try to be reset to the factory settings, yet hang on to what could be the problem, the cause, and the root of it all anyway. In order to rid ourselves of a dirty heart and horrible motives, we have got to check with the Creator on how to get back to the factory settings, and only He can do that.

We have to be able to walk away from the evil that we do not want to do and for which we do not want consequences. We have got to ask God to help us walk away. He said that He would provide us an escape, and besides providing us an escape, we have got to understand that we have to take the escape He provides. We cannot merely talk about an escape; we have to use the escape. We have got to be able to use the escape plan and get out of the way of the evil. Walk away.

There are times when I just want to say something to someone, then I realize that this is not going to go well. When you say these words, the consequence for saying these words are these actions right here. This is what's going to take place next. Have you ever done that? Where you really consider, now if I say this, she's going to say this in response, and when I do this, she's going to do this in response. And is the outcome that I want going to be this? Is this what I want the outcome to be? And everybody doesn't consider that. Everybody doesn't consider that to be something that is important to do. But I find it very important because at that particular point, you're in a relationship with this individual for a reason, and you're going to ruin the relationship while you're acting out of anger and frustration. Those are things that will cause you to sin. We want to be careful that we do not allow circumstances to cause us what I call "unscheduled" or "unforeseen" sin; things we cannot avoid.

One of my favorite passages of the Bible is Ephesians 4, verses 26 and 27. It reads, "In your anger do not sin, and do not let the sun fall on your wrath. Neither give place to the devil." That is quite the discipline for some of us. Some of us just cannot avoid anger, and sinning in the process, and part of the sin involves retaliation for something that is been done. We have got to get to a place where we do not do that. We have got to get to that place where that doesn't happen. We have got to get to a place where we can walk away from sin, and do not let those things that are designed to help us sin not to bother us at all.

How do you plan on that happening, Onedia? Well, I cannot tell you how I plan on it happening. What I can tell you is that I know it can happen; there is a way for it to take place. There's a way for you to avoid sin and please God, and not feel so taken advantage of. We have got to get past this point.

Verse 18 says, "I know that nothing good lives in me; that is in my sinful nature, for I have the desire to do what is good, but I cannot carry it out." That reminds us that we need God's help. We can only carry out what is good by the hand of God. We have to ask ourselves, what is it that I can get accomplished by myself? He says, apart from Me, you can do nothing. So what can I get accomplished by myself? And what is going to be required for me to take care of the will of God? We have got to ask that question. That question requires an answer as well.

We have got to look at ourselves and say, self, what is it that I need to do to be able to do this? What is it that I need to do? We have got to ask ourselves that question. And we have got to look at ourselves in a manner where we say to ourselves, well, you know what, this is what is required of us, so what are we going to do?

I just want us to be clear about the fact that at the end of every day, we have got to say to ourselves, how do I turn off this dirty heart and these horrible motives? How do I move forward to get past this point? And are we subconsciously hanging on to these horrible motives and this dirty heart because it is popular, because we have friends that have a dirty heart? All of that. How does this work, exactly? We have got to get to a point where we figure out how to stop that, how to stop wanting such a thing. How do we stop wanting that? How do we stop being motivated by it? Because at some point we are motivated by that; we are motivated by it. We are motivated by it. We are motivated by what we can do and how much influence we have with this dirty heart. It is something that we have; it is something that we have influence with and influence over. And whether that makes it right or not is an inconsequential conversation at this time, but it is clear that we need to investigate who we are in regard to this situation. Who are we? Who are we with this situation? Who are we? With a dirty heart and some horrible motives, who are we? Who do we turn into? Who do we become? How can we manage that process a little bit better, a little bit differently?

So, with a dirty heart and horrible motives, how we get past this point is this: number one, trust the Lord. Seek Him to get a clear understanding of what it is

He wants from you. Ask Him to help you figure out how to walk away. Ask Him to help you recognize better your escape plan. If He provides an escape for you, you're to ask Him, hey, how do I know it is Your plan? How do I know how to get past this point? We have got to get to that point where we can know just that: how to get past that point. How do we move beyond that piece?

Pray for a pure and clean heart; seek to pursue that. Know what that looks like. Know what your buttons are. My personal one is I cannot let little things get to me. I have to ask myself if I get distracted by this little detail, am I going to miss the whole goal? And the answer is yes. I love Paul's transparency in the text. I love how He confesses that, hey, even I have struggled with sin, and I know how you feel because I do what I do not want to do, and I do what I shouldn't do. I understand that, and I appreciate you, with a dirty heart and horrible motives.

Amen.

Lord God, we thank You afresh today for this word. We thank You for pulling on our hearts and tugging at our heartstrings to make us understand exactly what You would have for us to do. Lord God, we thank You right now because You are God and God alone, and You can help us with this situation. You can help us with exactly what You want us to do. And so, Lord God, right now I thank You that You are going to give us exactly what You would have for us, and exactly what You need for us to do to make it in this life and in this day-to-day walk we have, this struggle that we have. Oh Lord, I thank You right now that you're going to do exactly what we need. You're going to give us exactly what we need to make it every day, and be able to walk away from our dirty heart and our horrible motives. And should they return, Lord God, You're going to give us the ability to purge that again. Oh Lord God, afresh we thank You right now, and it is in Your son Jesus' name we pray and ask You these blessings. Amen.

ACKNOWLEDGEMENTS

God, thank You for Your plans for me. Thank You for *Living A Whole Life* and choosing me to complete Your project. I just want to please You. Thank You for continuing to anoint me and to invest in me and my gifts, which keep surprising me. Thank You for loving and forgiving me.

Hillary and Nehemiah, thank you for supporting me and my endeavors. Thank you for loving me, especially when I do nothing without a pen and a clipboard, thank you for enduring my late nights, your ideas, the sounding board, the love and the support. Thank you for celebrating our legacy.

Kimberly 'Ann' Joiner, thank you for reading my work and offering your honest feedback. May your life be blessed for doing God's will.

To my prayer partners and to my accountability partners, thank you for the long talks and the powerful prayers and the encouragement. To my pastor and church family, thank you so much for your love and support.

Minister Onedia N. Gage seeks to share her outlandish pursuit of God with her prayers, study and meditation. She desires to share her faith in a manner which helps you do the same through her calling. She hopes that these words bless you.

Please feel free to contact and share your testimony. onediagage@onediagage.com, or @onediangage (twitter). www.onediagage.com

Blogtalkradio.com/onediagage

Youtube.com/onediagage10

Facebook.com/onedia-gage-ministries

PREACHER ♦ ADVOCATE ♦ TEACHER ♦ FACILITATOR

CONFERENCE SPEAKER ♦ WORKSHOP LEADER

To invite Rev. Gage to speak at your church, women's ministry,

Or any other ministry.

Please contact us at: www.onedigage.com

@onediangage (twitter) ♦ onediagage@onediagage.com ♦ facebook.com/onediagageministries

youtube.com/onediagage ♦ blogtalkradio.com/onediagage ♦ ongage (Instagram)

Publishing

Do you have a book you want to write, but do not know what to do?

Do you have a book you need to publish but do not know how to start?

Would publishing move your career forward?

Let us help

onediagage@purpleink.net ♦ www.purpleink.net

281.740.5143 ♦ 512.715.4243

www.ingramcontent.com/pod-product-compliance
Lightning Source LLC
Chambersburg PA
CBHW071611080526
44588CB00010B/1093